INTERPRETING CHRIST

INTERPRETING CHRIST

Ernest Best

T&T CLARK
EDINBURGH

T&T CLARK
59 GEORGE STREET
EDINBURGH EH2 2LQ
SCOTLAND

First published 1993

ISBN 0 567 29215 0

British Library Cataloguing-in-Publication Data
A catalogue record for this book
is available from the British Library

Typeset by Trinity Typesetting, Edinburgh
Printed and bound in Great Britain by Biddles Ltd, Surrey

CONTENTS

ACKNOWLEDGEMENTS

'Scripture, Tradition and the Canon of the New Testament', The Manson Memorial Lecture for 1978, *The Bulletin of the John Rylands University Library of Manchester*, vol. 61, 1979, pp. 258-289.

'Interpreting the New Testament and Interpreting Christ', *Irish Biblical Studies*, vol. 3, 1981, pp. 2-14.

'On Defining the Central Message of the New Testament', The Ethel M. Wood Lecture for 1986, University of London Press.

'The Literal Meaning of Scripture, the Historical Critical Method and the Interpretation of Scripture', *The Proceedings of the Irish Biblical Association*, vol. 5, 1981, pp. 14-35.

'Exorcism in the New Testament and Today', *Biblical Theology*, vol. 27, 1977, pp. 1-8.

'The Interpretation of Tongues', *The Scottish Journal of Theology*, vol. 28, 1975, pp. 45-62 and T& T Clark Ltd.

'The Commentators and the Gospels' *The Expository Times*, vol. 79, pp. 260-4 and T& T Clark Ltd.

'Fashions in Exegesis: Ephesians 1:3' from *Scripture: Meaning and Method* (Essays presented to Anthony Tyrell Hanson, ed. by Barry P. Thompson) Hull University Press, 1987, pp. 79-81.

ABBREVIATIONS

CR	*Corpus Reformatorum*
Exp. T.	*Expository Times*
EvT	*Evangelische Theologie*
G.C.S.,	*Griechische christliche Schriftsteller*
H.T.R.	*Havard Theological Review.*
J.T.S.	*Journal of Theological STudies.*
MPG	Patrologia, Series Graeca, ed J.P. Migne.
MPL	Patrologia, Series Latina, ed J.P. Migne.
N.T.S.	*New Testament Studies*
S.J.T.	*Scottish Journal of Theology*
St. Th.	*Studia Theologica.*
WA	Luthers Werke (Weimarer Ausgabe)
WADB	WA, Die Deutsche Bibel.

INTRODUCTION

I have brought together here a number of studies written over
a period of years but all relating in some way to the interpretation of Scripture, particularly of the new Testament. They
include both attempts at the practice of interpretation and
studies of the theory of interpretation. It is then a collection of
essays centering on interpretation and not a systematic handbook of hermeneutics; some of these handbooks I find very
dull, for they are often laden with portentous words peculiar
to their authors, and make one wonder if those authors have
ever actually tried to interpret texts for the benefit of others.
For almost twenty years I worked in parish situations and was
compelled therefore to go beyond what a text actually said (and
determining that is not such a simple matter!) to its application
to a particular congregation at a particular time. I became
interested then in what I was actually doing when I expounded
Scripture and that interest has remained with me, which is not
to say that I was a successful interpreter or understood then or
now what I was attempting to do.

These 'essays' came into being in a number of different ways.
Some, in particular those on exorcism and glossolalia, because
at the time of their writing their subjects were receiving
widespread attention and the areas with which they dealt
involved New Testament themes; they represent attempts to
see the relevance of their themes for the church today. In the
same way, though not reproduced here, the final chapter of my

commentary on 1 and 2 Thessalonians[1] was an attempt to look at the continuing importance of the idea of the return of Christ and its possible significance or reinterpretation for today. It must be accepted, though it may seem regrettable, that sometimes detailed examination of a Scriptural theme leads to the negative conclusion that it should not be re-interpreted because it is no longer relevant to our time and culture, for us that of the late twentieth century western world, though perhaps still relevant to other cultures. Chapters 8-10 of 1 Corinthians fall into this category; nowhere in today's western world does food sacrificed to idols form a problem for believers; it undoubtedly still remains such for new Christians in many third world countries and therefore it is still *for them* an important part of Scripture, though it may not be for us.

When we start to look for the meaning of themes or passages today we require to remember always that in addition to all the normal environmental and cultural changes between our age and that of the New Testament one of the most significant is the existence of the New Testament itself. While some of its later writers may have known its earlier parts it had not become canonical or authoritative for them. Once people accord it a special place in their thought then it necessarily exercises a drawing power on them to accept its particular solutions to their problems. If believers spoke in tongues in the early days, and this is recorded in Scripture, then they ought to do so now. Going beyond this it is also true that any interpretation of a passage today begins with the loaded agenda of the various interpretations which it has received in the course of history.

Other articles reproduced here have been developments of my normal lecturing and represent attempts to examine some areas more closely. Some have been offshoots from something I have been writing but which would have been too extensive

[1] *I & II Thessalonians*, A. & C. Black, London, 1972, pp. 359-371.

to be included in the original writing. Into this last category falls my study of Eph. 1.3, 'Fashions in Exegesis', which surveys how the interpretation of one verse has changed through the centuries. In this connection it is interesting to observe how not merely the nature of the interpretation of verses and passages has changed with the passage of time but how even the extent of material devoted to them in commentaries has varied with time and theological orientation. It is easy to observe how changes in theological climate have led to alterations in interpretation; anyone who doubts this should examine the variations in the rendering of 1 Cor. 3.9 in the RSV, the Common Bible and the NRSV (translation is of course a form of interpretation). But it is also true that the general cultural climate affects interpretation. One factor leading to changes in interpretation of Eph. 1.3 was the alteration in philosophical outlook. The interest in history which developed in the nineteenth century accounts for much of the change between Matthew Henry and later commentators (see 'The Commentators and the Gospels'). In addition the more recent commentators were able to use new techniques, those of Source, Form and Redaction Criticism. In the period since that paper was written rhetorical criticism has been introduced as a new technique, and if the paper was to be updated more recent commentaries which have used that technique would require to be discussed.

So far as commentators go they are at a great disadvantage when compared with systematic theologians and preachers both of whom can simply ignore verses and passages which either they do not like or with whose content they disagree and work only with those that please them. Yet commentators also fail by evading issues. In Eph. 4.25 the writer, using a text from Zech. 8.16 which deals with truth between neighbours, exhorts his hearers to speak the truth because they are members one of another, a clear allusion to the church as the body of

Christ. He thereby implicitly equates being a neighbour with being a member of the church. In one sense this is satisfactory for he believes that the church is the true Israel and in Israel neighbour was another Jew, but in another it is not; Jerome pointed out many centuries ago that such an understanding conflicts with Jesus' definition of neighbour, and leads to the question: Is it not as necessary to speak the truth to non-Christians as to Christians? Jerome's observation is inconvenient for it casts a bad light on Ephesians; the result has been that the vast majority of its commentators have simply ignored the difficulty Jerome perceived.

For years I taught a course on the history of the interpretation of Scripture and this compelled me to explore in greater depth certain areas of interpretation and the methods people use in interpretation. The brief paper 'Paul and Thecla' was designed in connection with teaching to illustrate for students how the presuppositions of commentators dictate their results; to do this it seemed easiest to compose an extra couple of verses to a chapter in Acts and base my remarks on these; in that way I could make sure that students did not come with minds already made up as to what the passage meant and with the loaded agenda of earlier interpretations, and that at the same time all the views I wished to cover could be introduced in relation to one text. The words I have put into the mouths of commentators express the kind of sentiments I believe they would have used had they known the verses.

The variation in the meaning different commentators extract from the same passage has always fascinated me; having been brought up in a scientific tradition where it is expected that if faced with the same facts the same conclusions would be reached the shock of discovering that honest interpreters facing the same set of words could reach widely differing understandings has kept me continually reflecting on its significance. Gradually I have come to see how much readers themselves are involved in the process of interpretation. Even if they agree on what the words meant when they were written, and they rarely do, they still find difficulty in agreeing on how they are to be explained in relation to life today. This applies to synchronic readings of the text just as much as to traditional historical-critical exegesis. That the presuppositions of the interpreter are at work in synchronic reading can easily be seen when we examine the results of two different scholars subjecting the same text to that type of interpretation.

Synchronic reading of texts is not however as new as some of its exponents think, though it has received a new emphasis today. Whenever readers seek the understanding of a difficult word or phrase from its use at other points in the text or when they discover chiastic patterns in the text they are reading synchronically, and they have been doing this from the beginning. More importantly even when texts are thought to be read synchronically diachronic reading also enters. Words do not exist in a vacuum but belong to cultures. Their meanings vary with time and place. 'Biscuit' has different meanings on the two sides of the Atlantic. The meaning of 'gay' thirty years ago is now completely changed (compare the alteration in the meaning of 'prevent' from Elizabethan days). If we are to understand a text which incorporates such words we need to know where and when it was written. The importance of purely synchronic reading for the Christian interpretation of the New Testament is however doubtful since the people and events enshrined in the text have a special significance for Christians and cannot be isolated from their position in history.

Before any interpretation can take place at least one basic and fundamental question has to be faced: What is it which is to be interpreted? This can be looked at from at least two different angles. The first relates to the actual Christian writings to be examined. 1 Corinthians has been studied at much greater length and in much greater detail than 1 Clement; this implies the greater importance of the former for Christians, though not necessarily for historians, and immediately raises the question of the content of the canon. Should it consist of the books which are normally bound together to form the New Testament, or should a selection of these be treated as more essential than the remainder and as therefore forming the true canon (a canon within the canon), or should further writings be added (cf. the Mormons) for a proper conspectus? To explore this I wrote 'Scripture, Tradition and the Canon of the New Testament', the Manson Memorial Lecture for 1979. It was written at more or less the same time as my *From Text to Sermon*;[2] Christians need to know what they use as the basis of their faith and why they use it, and the lecture was an attempt to answer such questions. Implicit however is another question about the function of Scripture in determining what should be believed. This leads on to the other angle, to the question of what is to be interpreted, an angle which is even more fundamental. Once the question of the actual writings to be interpreted has been settled there remains the underlying issue of what is being interpreted. Is it the words of the books of the New Testament or what lies behind them and was the ultimate reason for their being written? If we read a number of accounts of the Battle of Waterloo do we read them to enjoy the accounts as literature or to understand the event of the battle which lies behind all of them and without which they would never have been written? Transferring this to the New Testament we have the question whether we are interpreting the words of its books or the person or event which led to their appearance? In fact of course it is not possible in our case to isolate these two aspects of original event, or supposed original event, and what is

---

[2] 2nd edn., T&T Clark, Edinburgh, 1988; see Chapter 1.

written about it, since the writings of the New Testament are the earliest access which we have to Jesus and more or less all else that has been written about him since then depends on them. If we wish to interpret him then we must also interpret these writings. It is to this basic issue that the paper 'Interpreting the New Testament and Interpreting Christ' is directed, and from which the title of this volume is derived.

Teachers of the New Testament are repeatedly asked, perhaps more often implicitly than explicitly, to sum up its message in a few sentences, which can then serve as a guide to belief and action. Is it then possible to isolate a core or centre which will adequately summarise what the New Testament says? If 'Jesus' is too imprecise as an answer can a better be formulated? In the Ethel M. Wood Lecture of 1986, 'On Defining the Central Message of the New Testament,' I looked at some of the attempts which have been made to give precision to the core of the New Testament. Were I rewriting this now I should want to emphasise more than I did then the difficulty created by the narrative nature of much of the New Testament. In each of the attempts that have been made to isolate the core special factors appear to have entered, either from the theological atmosphere of the time or its general cultural climate, and controlled each particular expression of the core, just as much as in the case of the interpretation of individual texts and passages.

The paper 'The Literal Meaning of Scripture, the Historical Critical Method and the Interpretation of Scripture' emerged from my regular lecturing on the history of the interpretation of Scripture. The reformers reacted strongly against the use of allegorical methods and sought to justify an approach which limited itself to the 'simple', 'plain', or literal meaning. What led them to this approach and how did they understand it? Since so much modern Protestant exegesis of the Bible from the conservative side and at popular level emphasises the same approach as alone valid and would, perhaps unconsciously, regard what was obtained through it as the meaning of Scripture for today, it is important to understand its origin, its weaknesses and strengths, and to fit it in to the general history of interpretation. Much preaching, also, when it does not allegorise passages tends to assume that what the literal meaning of the text says is the meaning for today. Yet even here there are variations in the degree to which the literal meaning of the text is acceptable. There are those who on the grounds of Scripture reject female ministers but do not object to women praying in a mixed group; others object to the latter practice but would permit them to worship with heads uncovered; others demand covered heads but allow the paying of interest on house mortgages despite the rejection of usury in Lev. 25.35-38. There are then degrees of acceptance of the literal meaning. As that example demonstrates the determination of the literal meaning is one thing and its practical acceptance as a basis for action in daily living quite another.

Part of the error in this approach is the isolation of particular statements in Scripture and their treatment as invariable propositions. This can lead to contrary advice on conduct. In Mark 10.17-22 Jesus tells the man who wishes to join him as a disciple that it is necessary to sell all his possessions and give the proceeds to the poor and that implies that the proceeds are not to be brought into the community for its use. In Acts 4.34-37 (cf. 2.45; 5.1-2) disciples sell their possessions and devote what results to the needs of the community. Are then Christians to direct their charitable givings to all people or only to other Christians? Scripture is in fact not a set of propositions but a series of reactions written by those who know Christ (not necessarily physically) and/or are inspired by the Holy Spirit and are addressed to particular situations. A text needs then not only to be understood in its immediate context but also in that of the whole Scripture; to ignore some of the primary witnesses which compose Scripture may in fact result in the isolation of the text from Christ.

This problem of the resolution of the meaning of particular texts might be easily solved if we had some standard against which to test possible conclusions. Various guidelines or standards have at times been suggested. If the proposed interpretation and/or action is contrary to sound reasoning it should not be accepted. On the other hand if it is in accord with what we see to be the core or central message of the New Testament, or with our preferred canon within the canon, then it can be accepted and acted on. Yet the formulation of the New Testament core is difficult and not all agree whether there should be a canon within the canon, and if there is in what it consists. As for 'sound reasoning' it functions better as a negative guide than a positive standard. Some would object to such questions as these being even raised and argue that criticism of the content of Scripture is not permissible. Yet as we have seen the determination of the original meaning, i.e. the content, is not itself a neutral matter but involves the total outlook of the interpreter. The negative attitude to criticism of the content of Scripture has always been stronger in Anglo-Saxon theology than in German Lutheran, probably because Luther through his criticism of the Epistle of James did criticise the content of Scripture and thus made it easier for his successors to do so in respect of other parts of Scripture. If we take seriously the question of the acceptance of what is in Scripture as authority for us then a part of the interpretation will always involve the examination of the result to see if it is in accord with what Christians believe (assuming that it is Christians who are interpreting). In the final issue it is not the relevance of the result of interpretation which is important but its truth.

The final paper in this collection and the most recently written, 'Off the Peg or Made to Measure', sets out to explore the ways which were open to the early Christians as they attempted to explain Jesus; there were not only existing categories into which he could be fitted but new categories emerging from the actual situations in which and to which he was being explained. Are there then open to us new ways of explaining him (and of course God and the Holy Spirit) which do not necessarily use biblical terms but concepts drawn from our contemporary situation? A prior question is clearly whether interpreters are restricted to the terms of Scripture. In fact no such restriction can be enforced. Anyone listening to the most conservative of interpreters soon finds that they use imagery not found in the Bible in order to explain what is in the Bible. More generally, since the situation of those who wish to understand Jesus varies considerably there could be many new ways of doing this, some arising out of the more immediate circumstances of a congregation and some out of the more general cultural situation.

There will be those who read these essays and think I ought to have gone further and carried out some actual positive interpreting. One of the main arguments however of what I have written has been the relation of interpretation to its context. What interpreters set out to explain belongs to its situation but they also belong to theirs and their interpretation is continually affected by their situation. Interpretation always takes place within a context. This context may be a very limited one as when preachers explain and apply passages to particular congregations; these are always being addressed at particular points in their history and particular settings in their surrounding environment. In these articles however I have not been addressing myself to small and limited particular groups. To develop interpretation in that way is too individualistic a task for the kind of studies I have been attempting, though I have to do it every time I preach. There are, however, wider situations which may be more properly described as cultural.

Are not some interpretations so general that they fit every possible cultural situation? When we call God 'Father' and Jesus 'Son' do we not use universal concepts understood by everyone? Yet there are languages in which no words exist for either father or son and these terms will be inadequate in such cultures. But where these words exist they offer useful categories and enable the ordinary person to grasp something of the meaning of the relationship of God and Christ. When however we try to examine more deeply the significance of the father-son relationship as applied to God and Christ we run into difficulties. As they have been understood in the past the terms imply 'maleness' in both God and Jesus. Perhaps this might be eliminated by speaking of mother and daughter or of parent and child. The former of these may indeed throw fresh light on the relationship of God and Christ, yet the relationship is still biological, and Christian theologians have always sought to eliminate this aspect by the use of terms like 'unbegotten'.

The seemingly universal terms in which Christ has been interpreted in the past have always, as we can now see with hindsight, been appropriate to the general cultural situation of their time and environment and there is no invariable interpretation valid at all times and in all cultures. But is there then an interpretation which is appropriate to western civilisation? Are there not generalisations which can be made of Christ which are valid for a large number of congregations and even also of countries? The answer ought to be 'Yes', yet when we examine the interpretations that are being made today, and there have been many, we quickly discover that they differ among themselves simply because culture is no longer as uniform as it once was. In the great majority of congregations there will be some who will object to a male oriented explanation of God, and even where a non-male oriented interpretation, if offered in the western world, might be acceptable to many congregations, the interpretation produced by liberation theology would be considered wrong, or at best irrelevant, in Western society. Environmentalist interpretations have not yet begun to have much effect but they are bound to appear increasingly in the future.

There is a further and I believe more important point. It is the rare biblical scholar who is equipped to provide an overall understanding. A Bultmann may do it for his generation, but it needs to be done over and over again for every generation. Those who would attempt it need to operate from within a thoroughly worked out philosophical and theological framework. Perhaps this is why some of the best interpretation at a wide level comes today from Catholic scholars, for most of these have had a deep grounding in dogmatic theology and philosophy. The great majority of biblical scholars would make no claim to work from a clearly thought out theological and philosophical framework. They find it difficult enough to keep up with some limited area within their own subject, perhaps a sub-section of Pauline studies, and also absorb the new understandings thrown on their chosen area by new discoveries (Qmran, Nag Hammadi), to find the time to know current theological, sociological and theological trends, let alone to empathise with the thought and feeling currents of the outside (i.e. outside the academic) world. Interpretation also always involves an element of what may be loosely called 'imagination'; the slow grind of understanding texts against their own background leaves exegetes little time for its play, and indeed may even inhibit its exercise.

But even if exegetes as exegetes are not equipped for the wider role of interpreter they still have an important function to fulfil in the understanding of Scripture. When new interpretations appear it is their task to show whether these interpretations are continuous with those that have emerged earlier and been acceptable as faithful to Scripture. They do not have to judge whether the new interpretation is the same or similar to what is found in Scripture; they cannot do that for they themselves vary in their determination of the original or historical meaning. In any case if the meaning put before them for their approval is to be a genuinely new understanding for a new culture it will not be expressed in the same, or even similar, language to any section of the original New Testament. Does it however remain faithful to the core in so far as that core can be detected? The proper role of exegetes *qua* exegetes is thus primarily negative. As exegetes they cannot lay down in advance what the interpretation in a particular situation will be. They can only look at what others through their imagination and their historical, sociological, philosophical and theological knowledge have suggested and check it out. Their function is primarily critical rather than exploratory, though there have been exegetes who have explored new paths, not simply new paths in interpreting the original words, but new paths in understanding their ultimate meaning.

In conclusion may I apologise because there is a considerable overlap at times between the various essays; anyone who has had to lecture to different audiences about the same wide subject, though dealing at any particular time only with a limited area within it, will appreciate that there are preliminary generalities which need to be enunciated each time. If this had been a systematic handbook on interpretation these repetitions could have been eliminated. In fact the only alterations made to the original publications have been necessary cross referencing and the expurgation of typographical and other minor errors.

As I proofread these essays I became aware that they themselves show situational orientation. The earlier ones were written prior to the need in Britain to avoid sexist language, in the later ones more care is taken over the use of term 'men' and masculine personal pronouns; I have not altered the earlier essays to conform to normal present day usage and the essays therefore provide an example of what I am in part getting at.

1

SCRIPTURE, TRADITION AND THE CANON
OF THE NEW TESTAMENT[1]

The problem of the canon exists only for the church. The historian who is interested in first-century Christianity would probably select as his most important documents many of those which comprise the canon of the new Testament, but they would offer for him no problems of authority or uniqueness. If, however, the Christian is asked why these books are important he will not just reply that it is because they are the earliest about his religion, or the most free from later editorial contamination. If Pilate's 'diary of Holy Week', though he would not have described it in that way, were to be discovered this would be of great interest to the historian but it is improbable that it would ever become part of the canon. Why should the twenty-seven books of the New Testament have obtained a special position within the church, be treated as norms, read Sunday by Sunday in the liturgy, used as sources for texts for sermons?

In looking at these questions I am not primarily interested in determining which books belong to the canon, or in

---

[1]The Manson Memorial Lecture delivered in the University of Manchester on 14th November 1978. So far as I can detect, T. W. Manson never published anything dealing directly with the issues I am about to discuss. There are periods when certain problems come to the fore; during this time the one with which I deal lay dormant; today those who like him attempt to hold together their academic integrity and Christian faith are forced to look anew at the question of the canon. Though I cannot claim to be either as good as scholar or as loyal a churchman as he was I offer this to his memory.

deciding at what period and for what reason a particular book came to be accepted, but instead in the question of the fact or existence of the canon. Canon and norm go together. How, however, can a book which uses a great deal of mythological language, and that not only about seemingly peripheral matters like the heavenly powers, but even also about its central figure, be a norm for a world which is rapidly increasing the areas of life from which mythological language is excluded? How also can a book be a norm for an age which is concerned with issues like abortion and the termination of life, with industrial disputes and the exhaustion of the world's energy resources, issues with which the book itself never apparently deals? If Christians are interested in the New Testament as a norm they are not interested in it as a norm for the middle of the second or for the fourth century, depending on when it is thought to have become the canon, but as a norm for the twentieth and the twenty-fifth century.

With this kind of question in mind I wish to set the problem of the canon in relation to the problem of scripture. Within the last one hundred and fifty years much work has been done on the writings which comprise the New Testament canon. We now know fairly clearly when each was written, who may have written it and who probably did not, and what circumstances produced it. If the early church had had the benefit of our wisdom it might well have made different judgments in its selection. If it had been properly aware of the non-Petrine authorship of 2 Peter and if it had had Luther's insight into the unorthodoxy of James we might have had a smaller canon. It is not, however, questions of that type which are to be examined here, but the more basic issue: how has a changed understanding of scripture affected our understanding of scripture as *canon*?

We begin with Mark iv. 1-20. It is generally accepted that this section of Mark has passed through at least three stages: the original parable (vv. 3-8) which was almost certainly part of the genuine Jesus-tradition; secondly, the addition of the interpretation (vv. 14-20); thirdly, the insertion of the brief intervening section (vv. 10-12) in which a reason is given for the telling of parables. Let us look at it in a little more detail beginning with the text as we now possess it. Again it is generally agreed that certain parts of the text come from Mark's own hand. In particular, the introduction (vv. 1, 2):

> 'Again he began to teach beside the sea. And a very large crowd gathered about him, so that he got into a boat and sat in it on the sea; and the whole crowd was beside the sea on the land. And he taught them many things in parables, and in his teaching he said to them.'

It is probable that verse 9, 'And he said, He who has ears to hear, let him hear,' has also been given its present position by Mark, though the saying itself may go back to Jesus.

Verses 10-12 contain considerable evidence of Mark's hand. Opinions differ whether he created the saying,

> 'To you has been given the secret of the Kingdom of God, but for those outside everything is in parables; so that they may indeed see, but not perceive and may indeed hear, but not understand; lest they should turn again, and be forgiven,'

or took from the tradition a saying which did not originally refer to 'parables' in our sense and applied it to them. In any case, the present position of the saying and its relation to the parable are due to Mark.[1] Probably also most of verse 10, 'And when he was alone, those who were about him with the twelve asked him concerning the parables,' comes from Mark. Mark was able to insert the difficult saying of verses 11 and 12 between the parable[2] and the interpretation because the interpretation did not exactly fit the parable. The saying does harmonise, however, with the emphasis that Mark elsewhere

---

[1] The present argument for three stages in the development would not be affected if it was held the saying gained its present position in the pre-Markan tradition.

[2] The form in Mark iv. 3-8 may not be precisely the original form; it makes no essential difference to the argument if it was briefer.

lays on Jesus' private teaching of the disciples,[1] and it stresses that the interpretation can only be understood by those who are within the church.

Setting aside now Mark's particular theory of the parables which he applied to this parable, we move back one stage to that interpretation which describes the varied reaction of those who have heard the Gospel. Curiously most recent commentaries on Mark, while they discuss in detail the original meaning of the parable, and Mark's particular theory of parables, deal very briefly with this interpretation as if they did not think it important.[2] As for the original parable, it is unnecessary to sketch the various theories that have been applied to it. We clearly do not possess it within the context of its original setting. Many commentators used to take it as Jesus' own explanation of the progress of his preaching; after his ministry in Galilee had gone on for some time he saw that there were some who had listened to him for a while and then for various reasons dropped out, but there were a certain number who had continued with him. More generally today the explanation of Jeremias is accepted; the parable relates to the certainty of the harvest which will be the Kingdom of God; though some fail an abundant harvest will ensue.[3]

Many years ago I heard a distinguished New Testament scholar give a series of lectures on the parables. He spent a long time explaining this parable along the lines of Jeremias. He paid no attention to the interpretation and only dealt with the difficult saying in verses 11 and 12 in order to dismiss it in its present form from the genuine Jesus-tradition. This raised in my mind the question: if scripture is authoritative as the lecturer assumed and if the interpretation of either verses 14-

---

[1] Often, after Jesus has taught the crowds, he retires privately with the disciples and explains to them his teaching (vii. 17 ff.; viii. 14-21; ix. 28 f.; ix. 33 ff.; x. 10-12).

[2] There are honourable exceptions, e.g. C. E. B. Cranfield.

[3] *The Parables of Jesus* (London, 1963), pp. 149-51.

20 or the difficult saying of verses 11 and 12 is how scripture
understood the parable, have we any right to go back and ask
after an original meaning of which we cannot even be sure and
then make it the basis of our exposition? Between the original
telling of the parable by Jesus and its present use in Mark there
lies a developing tradition in which there were at least three
stages, and there may have been more. Have we to understand
the parable only in the way in which it is explained and used
in Mark? Or have we to understand it as it was explained by the
oral tradition where it was associated with the interpretation of
verses 14-20? Or have we to seek a meaning which was the
original meaning in the life of Jesus? The difficulty for many
is increased because theologically they find Mark's explanation
almost impossible to accept. The second stage, parable plus
church interpretation, seems satisfactory though many again
are unhappy with the differences which exist between the
parable and the church interpretation. So far as the stage in the
life of Jesus is concerned, while Jeremias may be right, no one
can really be wholly convinced of this. The problem is increased because there were further stages in the development
of the tradition. J. D. Kingsbury relates the form in Matthew
to the question of the success of the Christian mission to the
Jewish community.[1] In 1 Clement xxiv the language of the
parable seems to be merged with a concept which comes from
other parts of scripture, Jesus as the seed who is sown into the
ground, who dies and rises to new life. Though 1 Clement lies
outside the canon why should this not be taken as a penetrating
and valid interpretation and ascribed canonical authority?

Two further illustrations will make clearer the problem
created by the development of tradition. (1) It is generally
agreed that John in the composition of his gospel has used a

[1]J. D. Kingsbury, *The Parables of Jesus in Matthew 13: A Study in Redaction Criticism*
(London, 1969), pp. 22 ff.

source, written or oral, for the various signs which he recounts, and which he interprets. Many of those who have worked on this source argue that in it the miracles were used to glorify Jesus; he was set out as 'Divine Man'. Going behind that source we can be reasonably certain that some of the signs which it records occurred in some form in the life of Jesus. The healing of the blind man (ch. 9) will serve as example. If Jesus healed this man, then he did so because of his compassion for the man; he did not treat him primarily as an object to be used in a lesson to the crowds or the disciples; he saw the man's need and the man for his part was willing to respond to Jesus' love. Then in the tradition of the signs source the story was used to proclaim the power of Jesus. Finally John took it and used it as a sign that Jesus opens blind minds. Again, there are a number of stages of development. Which is authoritative? (2) The parable of the lost sheep: in Luke 15 this is a story of the love of God for the sinner who has gone astray and whom the Pharisees would leave to his fate and it tells of the joy in heaven over the discovery of the sheep and the sinner's repentance. In Matthew 18 the same parable is used, not to emphasise the sinner's return but the qualities of a good pastor; he should be looking for lost sheep. Which understanding is authoritative?

The problem raised here can be seen in another way in the interrelation of the different books of the New Testament. Matthew and Luke use Mark; if we do not go back to the tradition at the pre-Markan stage and select it in preference to Mark should we not eliminate Mark and use only Matthew and Luke? Alternatively we might separate out their sources and canonize Mark, Q, special Matthew and special Luke. Second Peter largely incorporates Jude and so depends on it. Could we not then do without Jude? Quite apart from any idea that we should move back to pre-written tradition, ought we not to trim down the canon by the omission of those writings which depend on others and perhaps incorporate them? To do so would, of course, be to create a canon within the canon, but that in other ways is a solution which has often been adopted.

Cannot a good case, however, be made out that the New Testament itself creates a canon within itself?[1] When Paul tells the Corinthians how they should keep the eucharist and says 'For I received from the Lord what I also delivered to you' (1 Cor. xi. 23), is he not setting up an authoritative standard or canon? Is this not also true when he recalls the same Corinthians to the primitive creed of 1 Corinthians xv. 3-5 and reminds them of particular eye-witnesses of the resurrection? when he tells them that it is not he himself but the Lord who has set down the standard for non-separation of husbands and wives (1 Cor. vii. 10; cf. ix. 14)? when he recalls the Thessalonians to the traditions which he and others have taught them (2 Thess. ii. 15)? Is Paul with these passages not acknowledging a canon and should we prefer him to what he himself sets out as norm and authority? Again the apostolic decrees of Acts 15, as Luke presents them,[2] have an authoritative position, as does the agreement between Paul and the Jerusalem leaders in Galatians ii. 1-10; they are decisions which are intended to rule the whole church. Paul himself may even function as canon when he tells his readers to imitate him (1 Cor. iv. 16; xi. 1).

The real question can now be isolated; why should that stage of the tradition which we call scripture be given an authoritative place in the church rather than some earlier or later stage within the tradition? Why not select on the one hand the pre-Pauline fragments or on the other the Nicene Creed, the Westminster Confession of Faith, the Councils of the Church up to and including Vatican II or the Lambeth Quadrilateral?

---

[1] Cf. S. Pedersen, 'Die Kanonfrage als historisches und theologisches Problem", *St. Th.*, xxxi (1977), 83-136; H. von Campenhausen, *The Formation of the Christian Bible* (London, 1972), pp. 106 ff.

[2] The original meaning and *Sitz im Leben* of these decrees are another matter. In Acts they clearly possess a universally authoritative position.

The problem is intensified because we find contradictions between portions of scripture. The differences between Paul and James have been argued out at length and in depth, and there is no need to rehearse them. A simpler difference will illustrate the issue. When Peter and John were brought before the Sanhedrin and were ordered to stop preaching about Jesus, they replied that they had to obey God rather than men (Acts iv. 19); when Paul writes to the Romans he tells them that the governing authorities have been instituted by God and that he who resists the authorities resists God. What are we to make of this? How can the canon be normative if it contains such differences? Is not unity of teaching a presupposition for normativeness?

It is necessary to look at the nature of the New Testament scriptures. Beginning with Jesus we have the development of traditions about him in narrative, hymn, creed and epistle. Scripture is the freezing of that tradition at particular points. It is as if someone were to take cross-sections of developing tradition at various periods. We have the cross-section which is given by Mark and then later cross-sections as given by Matthew, Luke and John. But the cross-sections do not follow one another in succession as if a tree trunk were sawn across at various points, each of which would reveal exactly the same pattern or rings. There was no uniform development of tradition. Instead, from the beginning the traditions were moving in a number of different directions. These different developments can be thought of as originating in the same source, but also as they grow as crossing one another. Thus the lines of tradition which run through Mark and Q meet again in both Luke and Matthew.[1] Each cross-section has also to be seen against the background of the community for which its author was writing. So seen some of the differences between

[1]The same conclusion results whatever solution we adopt to the synoptic problem.

the various points of the New Testament disappear. The different teachings about the state's authority and man's obedience arose out of the difference in situation as recounted in the early chapters of Acts and the situation, so far as we can gather it, in the Church of Rome to which Paul was writing (or possibly the church in Palestine if Romans represents Paul's speech for his defence in Jerusalem). Scripture is then the freezing of the tradition in particular contexts.[1]

But to say that scripture is the freezing of tradition in particular contexts requires some further explanation. In speaking of the writings of the New Testament or of the tradition as belonging to 'contexts' there are at least three elements which can be seen in the term 'context'. First there is 'situation', the circumstances which called forth the writing; in the case of 1 Corinthians these were a letter from Corinth and information supplied by visitors from the congregation there to Paul, together with his own personal position in Ephesus from which he was writing.[2] Second there is 'culture' — the general culture of the person by whom the letter was written and of the people to whom it was written; there were a number of such cultures in the ancient world of which for first-century Christianity the Jewish and the Hellenistic are particularly important. In any particular writing or freezing of tradition the culture of the writer and of the recipients need not be the same, though there will be little communication if their cultures do not to some extent overlap. Finally there is the particular

---

[1]For a fuller treatment of this view of scripture see my *From Text to Sermon* (2nd edn., T. & T. Clark, Edinburgh, 1988), pp. 11 ff.

[2]W. Marxsen, *The New Testament as the Church's Book* (Philadelphia, 1972), pp. 44 ff., writes of the 'New Testament as the Church's Earliest Extant Volume of Preaching' (p. 44). This is true in so far as the New Testament writings as freezings of the tradition are like sermons addressed to particular situations and bring to those situations God's Word. Marxsen clearly does not intend the terms 'sermon' and 'preaching' which he uses to be confined to the 'form' of what happens in the average pulpit on Sunday mornings; unfortunately the terms do not indicate the flow of the tradition into and out of the books of the New Testament and are for that reason not wholly satisfactory.

world-view, or theology, of the writer; no one's world-view coincides precisely with the culture in which he lives; due to his own experience and his own thinking he will always distance himself some way from the culture to which he belongs; the first-century Christians because of their experience distanced themselves very considerably from the cultures in which they lived; they were 'foreigners' in the world.[1]

The elements of the tradition with which we have largely dealt up to now were stories involving Jesus. The tradition was, however, also carried on through changing interpretations of his significance. This interpretative element is very strong in the passages which are isolated as primitive creeds and hymns. Three examples provide three different interpretations:

> '. . . how you turned to God from idols, to serve a living and true God, and to wait for his Son from heaven, whom he raised from the dead, Jesus who delivers us from the wrath to come (1 Thess. i. 9f.).'

Paul summarises here his initial preaching in Thessalonica, apparently in the words of an early creed. There is no reference in it to present redemption from sin, which many would consider the essence of Christianity, and there is too much emphasis on idols for it to be of any use in a culture where these are not normally found. The present reference to redemption appears in the best-known of these early creeds:

> 'Christ died for our sins in accordance with the Scriptures; he was buried; he was raised on the third day in accordance with the Scriptures; he appeared to Cephas, then to the twelve' (1 Cor. xv. 3-5).

Yet this itself has no reference to Christ's victory over evil and the devil; this is found implicitly in the Philippian hymn (ii. 6-11) and explicitly in many of the credal passages which refer to Christ's ascension, e.g.,

> [Christ] who has gone into heaven and is at the right hand of God, with angels, authorities, and powers subject to him' (1 Peter iii. 22).

---

[1]Cf. Phil, iii. 20 f.; 1 Pet. i. 1; ii. 11; Heb. xi. 13, etc.

This victory over the supernatural powers is found widely in the New Testament. Some of these primitive creeds and hymns were taken up and developed in the early church, but others, like that in 1 Thessalonians i. 9 f., led to dead ends and were dropped. The significance of Jesus is also, of course, drawn out in the Gospels and in the Epistles in a more extensive way. In the later church new creeds were developed and eventually themselves received authoritative position; they became in effect freezings of the tradition; the Nicene creed functions for many Christians as such an authoritative freezing. But each freezing is a freezing within a situation and a culture and none is an absolute freezing. Why then should we give authority to some of these situationally and culturally defined freezings and not to others? Why in particular are the freezings in scripture authoritative?[1] Why should this particular set of 'freezings' become a norm?

Before we proceed further, we may sum up the problem as it now appears: scripture recognises pre-scriptural material and accords it normative value; some post-scriptural material has normative value for some Christians and churches; scripture contains within itself diversity of outlook, if not direct contradiction. Why then should certain freezings which have taken place along the manifold lines of tradition be accorded normative value? To this we must add doubts about the reasoning which led to the original selection of writings as canonical; we recognise different senses in the way 'apostle' is used in the New Testament and therefore might make different judgments about the apostolicity of particular writings; we reach

---

[1]In speaking of scripture as the freezings of the tradition I am not intending to suggest that scripture is the record of a series of 'saving events'. Leaving aside altogether the question of what constitutes 'saving events', 'record' is too weak a word. Each writing of scripture is the response of a writer who stands within the corporate Christian experience and has a charisma of the Holy Spirit to a particular situation, not just a witness to something that has happened. Of course 'the something that has happened' (if that is the right way to express it) conditions the 'response'.

different conclusions about the authorship of the various writings; we often date their period of composition differently from what we believed when they were first accepted into the canon.

At this point a question must come up. Can we isolate and identify what it is which is frozen in scripture, or what it is which creates the stream of tradition?

Before we take up this question another illustration may help. There are two theories about the creation of the universe. One regards it as beginning with an initial event when all matter and energy were created; for the other, matter and energy are in course of continuous creation. In parallel to the latter it would be possible to hold a view in which tradition was being continuously created in the life of the church; this might be the position of those who believed that they had direct access through the Holy Spirit to Christ and who received in their minds from him fresh interpretations and teachings; this was indeed the view of some gnostics and of the Montanists in the second century. It might also be the position of those who set scripture and tradition alongside one another as independent or complementary sources of revelation, with tradition multiplying with the passage of time. According to the other view of creation what we have is a knowledge of the whole universe at a fixed position, i.e., today, and have to deduce from that given position how it began. The scientist assumes that the same laws have been valid throughout the life of the universe and that given sufficient time and a large enough computer he can work back to the original initial condition, or at least to a second after the original condition, though of course because it is such a gigantic problem he realises he may never actually do this. Christians have in the New Testament and in the later period of the church the tradition as it developed, and thus they know it at certain periods under certain conditions in certain contexts. But, as the Christian looks at it today, the data of the tradition do not always harmonise. He cannot therefore begin to feed the material in any straightforward kind of way into some kind of computer and come up with a result. Worse than this, while the scientist works with the universe as it now is and can make observations on its existing state to assist him to draw conclusions, the Christian has to work with material from which he is separated by almost two millennia. Another question comes up here: is there a sense in which what a Christian scholar is able to do is similar to the work of the scientist who only attempts to get back to a second after the beginning? The scientist *qua* scientist makes no claim to be able to decide what started the universe. The Christian scholar has no eye-witness accounts of the resurrection, but only reports of its effects on those who believed it to have taken place. As a historian he cannot get back beyond the 'second after', yet as Christian he must say something about the very beginning; unlike the scientist he cannot evade this.

Let us return now to the question raised a moment ago: what is it which is frozen within each section of the tradition? We can certainly give it names — the Gospel, the Word, the Kerygma. Each of these unfortunately carries a whole penumbra of meaning with it and is not nearly as simple as it sounds. When we try to answer a little more clearly, we may say that what we isolate is either a central doctrine or doctrines, an ur-Kerygma, or of a set of facts — Jesus was born in Nazareth, taught and healed, was crucified and rose again. The second of these, the set of facts, seems much the easier to tackle and indeed one can be reasonably sure of the truth of at least some of them. But how far does this take us? Christians do not believe merely in a set of facts, but at least in facts which have a certain understanding attached to them. In terms of 1 Corinthians xv. 3, it is not just 'Christ died' but 'Christ died for our sins'. Interpretations, however, always exist within

contexts; they are given by people and relate to their circumstances, cultures and world-views; any formulation of words
can only be understood by us in relation to our contexts and
if we formulate it we will always formulate it in relation to our
context; we can never disincarnate ourselves and become pure
neutral intelligence.

We can easily see that this is true when we look at the
attempts which have been made to isolate that which is frozen
and discover the 'essence' of Christianity.[1] In the course of
Christian history this has been done many times and the result
has been stated in many different ways: sometimes as the
central points of the teaching of Jesus — the Fatherhood of
God, the brotherhood of man, the immortality of the soul;
sometimes in terms of a picture of Jesus; sometimes as a
transactional soteriology — God in some way bore our sins in
Christ's death; sometimes in much vaguer terms as 'The man
for others'; sometimes in terms of discipleship as personal
devotion to Christ.[2] The simpler and more primitive the creed
the easier it seems to be to state it — 'Jesus is Lord'.[3] But apart
from the question of date,[4] 'Lord' is a word which has to be set
in a context; if one man says 'Jesus is Lord' instead of saying
'Caesar is Lord' and if another says 'Jesus is Lord' in the light
of 'Yahweh is Lord' they may be saying two quite different
things. Simplicity has its perils. The statements we produce
bear signs of our own times even though we suppose they are
absolutes. That they should bear the imprint of our own
culture and thought is in practice not bad but good; for if they
were not couched within such terms we would neither be able

---

[1]Harnack's *Das Wesen des Christentums* could be rendered 'The Essence of Christianity'.
[2]But James does not show much of this element while some 'heretical' writings do.
[3]Cf. G. Wainwright 'The New Testament as Canon', *S.J. T.*, xxviii (1975), 551-71; see pp.
556 and 561, n. 1.
[4]It is not necessarily the most primitive; this may have been 'Jesus is the Messiah'.

to understand them ourselves nor be capable of communicating them to others; but we should never treat them as absolutes.

We would thus agree with Nineham that there is no fixed or constant 'quantum of truth'[1] if by that he means there is no 'invariant' statement of that form which the tradition derives. But that is not to say that at the centre there is a 'black hole' or 'nothingness'.[2] What was an is there is that which is expressed in each of the primitive creeds and hymns, in the books of scripture, in the writings of Augustine, Thomas, Luther, Calvin and many others. It cannot be expressed in a formula that lasts for all time;[3] every expression of it is culturally

---

[1] Dennis Nineham, *The Use and Abuse of the Bible* (London, 1976), pp. 222, 230, etc. 'Quantum', with all its present-day associations in modern physics, seems an odd word to use. Truth does not come in discrete quanta, all similar in value to one another, nor does truth consist of a set of such quanta like separate propositions. In denying that it does Nineham is only stating the obvious and attacking what no one holds.

[2] It so happened when I was re-reading Nineham for the purpose of this lecture that I came on an article on fantasy in literature (J. H. Timmermann, 'Fantasy Literature's Evocative Power', *The Christian Century*, xcv, no. 17, 1978, 533-7). 'In order to characterise a work as fantasy literature, I would argue, there are six traits which must be present to some degree; story, common characters, evocation of another world, use of magic and the supernatural, a clear sense of good and evil, and the quest' (p. 534). All these would seem to be characteristics of scripture as Nineham describes it. How would Nineham argue that scripture does not fall under the category 'fantasy'? It does not seem that at any point he really raises the question of truth. It enters only by inference when he follows John Knox and represents the beginning as Jesus plus the early church (that is rather crudely put), where he would presumably argue that the experience of the first Christians was true.

[3] J. D. G. Dunn, *Unity and Diversity in the New Testament* (London, 1977) speaks of an 'irreducible minimum' (p. 376) instead of an 'invariant', but he does not distinguish the two terms sufficiently. His formulation of the irreducible minimum is in terms of the individualistic emphasis of Evangelical Protestantism: 'Christianity begins from and finally depends on the conviction that in Jesus we still have a paradigm for man's relation to God and man's relation to man, that in Jesus' life, death and life out of death we see the clearest and fullest embodiment of divine grace, of creative wisdom and power, that ever achieved historical actuality, that the Christian is accepted by God and enabled to love God and his neighbour by that same grace which we now recognize to have the character of that same Jesus' (p. 377). He formulates the unifying strand in the New Testament as 'the unity between the historical Jesus and the exalted Christ, that is to say, the conviction that the wandering charismatic preacher from Nazareth had ministered, died and been raised from the dead to bring God and man finally together, the recognition that the divine power through which they now worshipped and were encountered and accepted by God was one and the same person, Jesus,

conditions.[1]

Different schools of thought in history isolated different 'essences of Christianity' because they emphasised particular features within the whole, selecting some elements for attention and playing down others. In effect they created a canon within a canon. However, before we examine this concept we need to look in a little more detail at one problem for which the canon within a canon is sometimes put forward as a solution, namely, the differences and/or contradictions within scripture.[2] The reverse side of this problem is the unity of scripture. A generation ago it was customary to speak of *the* theology of the new Testament, now it is more customary to speak of a number of theologies within the New Testament. The problem of contradictions within scripture was at one stage historically important in relation to the canon since some of the second and third generation of reformed theologians used the contradictions which they alleged to exist between the Apocrypha of the Old Testament and the Old Testament itself as a reason for rejecting the canonicity of the Apocrypha.

It is possible to see quite quickly, at least in formal terms, from where contradictions and/or differences in scripture arise; out of the differing situations of the recipients, the differing cultures in which the New Testament was written,

---

the man, the Christ, the Son of God, the Lord, the life-giving Spirit' (p. 369). This latter statement seems to be conditioned by the modern theological debate about the continuity between Jesus and the primitive community and the interest in charismatic activity. I doubt if any of the writers of the New Testament would have understood him; some of them might have understood the earlier formulation of his irreducible minimum but rejected it. That both of these formulations are conditioned by our cultural heritage does not of itself mean that they are wrong, only that they are not invariant. The 'centre' has to be expressed in ways that do not deny but show knowledge of our cultural heritage, yet because our culture is continually changing any statement of the 'centre' must change.

[1] Cf. von Campenhausen, op. cit. p. 105.

[2] These have been set out in sober and restrained fashion by Dunn, op. cit. *passim.* A less balanced view is found in J. Charlot, *New Testament Disunity* (New York, 1970). Books which overplay the unity are common.

and the differing world-views of the writers; in the last we can include the lack of information or the mis-information possessed by the various writers.

To this last category belong the simple factual contradictions, e.g., the day of the cleansing of the temple (was it Sunday or Monday of Holy Week or neither?), the names of the twelve, the date of the passion. But, as the last example shows, it is not easy to be clear that this is just a simple factual contradiction, for the date of the crucifixion may have been deliberately altered at some stage in order to advance a particular theological interpretation. Within the terms of a modern critical view of the New Testament almost all these factual contradictions can be held to be unimportant. Yet clearly there are limits to factual contradiction: if there was a tradition that Jesus had never been put to death but had died in his sleep as an old man, this would be impossible to reconcile with the accounts we have. A second category of difference and/or contradiction relates to the area of ethical behaviour. We have already drawn attention to the difference which we find in Paul's attitude to governing authority in Romans xiii and the attitude which is shown by Peter and John in Acts iv when they were brought before the Sanhedrin. The Sanhedrin cannot be classed simply as a civil authority; it demands from John and Peter an acquiescence in a primarily religious decision, rather than in a primarily political decision such as the payment of taxes. Sometimes what appear to us to be contradictions may indeed only so appear because we are unaware of the full context. The differences which exist in Paul's attitude to women in 1 Corinthians xi and 1 Corinthians xiv (provided that xiv 34, 35 are part of the original text) require some considerable ingenuity if they are to be reconciled but if we knew more about Corinth it might be possible to harmonise them without difficulty. Again, however, few of the contradictions in this area seriously perturb thoughtful Christians today.

None, however, of these 'differences and/or contradictions' touches the 'substance of faith', whatever that may be. This could happen once we move into the area of doctrine where the problems become much greater. Certainly some of the differences within the New Testament are due to the development of theology within the first century. We find different christologies; there are places where an adoptionist position shows through against others where the pre-existence of Christ is assumed. Other differences within the area of doctrine are really of mixed category: the picture of Paul and his thought in Acts does not cohere in every respect with the picture in the genuine Pauline letters. More serious is the two-fold picture of the teaching and person of Jesus supplied by the synoptic gospels and the gospel of John. Scholars are able to live with this, but it can seriously disturb many lay Christians when they first become aware of it. Perhaps scholars get over their worries too easily! Historically, however, it has been the difference in attitude to God which we find in Paul and in James to which most attention has been given. Here is a difference which some, like Luther,[1] believe creates such a cleavage within the canon that it is impossible for both Paul and James to be taken as normative for faith and therefore one must be eliminated from it. It is not necessary here to argue that James can or cannot be reconciled with Paul but to draw attention to the basic question 'How far can contradictions exist within the canon without creating a cleavage therein?' If we are to draw a line between what is canonical and what is not we require a yardstick with which we may draw the line. This yardstick can either come from within the material or it can come from outside, or it may be derived from both.

[1] Whether Luther modified his earlier view on this is irrelevant to the present argument. For a detailed discussion of the development and significance of Luther's understanding, see I. Lønning, 'Kanon im Kanon' (Oslo and Munchen, 1972).

The canon as we know it is at least in part the result of the application of a yardstick from outside. In so far as the church in the fourth century formally drew up lists of books which it regarded as canonical, so distinguishing them from others, we have an external authority applied to create a distinction. For the moment, however, we set this aside, and look instead at the attempt to find in scripture a core or a principle which permits the drawing of lines between what is authoritative and what is not. Is there a canon within a canon? Before examining this in detail it is well to recognise that in actual fact almost every Christian operates, perhaps unconsciously, in terms of a canon within a canon. Preachers have only to look at their collection of sermons to know that there are some writings in the New Testament from which they preach more often and with which they are happier than others.

The existence of a canon within the canon has been solved in different ways. (*a*) Some have looked on the canon as a list having a hard core with a soft edge; when they looked back into the history of how and when the twenty-seven books were chosen they saw that there was general agreement on all except seven, viz. Hebrews, James, 2 Peter, 2 and 3 John, Jude, Revelation, and these were the soft edge. (*b*) Others have approached the problem by choosing a particular author or authors as the centre. It could be argued that the present canon itself was selected in this way through choice from the extant writings of books by apostolic authors. Many Protestants, though they might not state it formally in these terms, would choose those parts of the New Testament which agreed with Paul as being the true or inner canon. Many liberals chose Jesus, made his teaching central and judged everything else in its light. Carlstadt approached this position in so far as he set the gospels and Acts in the highest of his categories of New Testament books. Certain publishers of the Bible do this when they print the sayings of Jesus in red letters. At least one difficulty in choosing the sayings of Jesus as the essential canon lies in our uncertainty in determining what were his actual words. (*c*) Some would like to unearth an 'earliest kerygma'. Those who have opted for this have not themselves agreed on what it was.[1] (*d*) Others choose a principle, that of justifying grace, or that which is existential and cannot be demythologised. In modern discussions of the inner canon these are often associated. On the one hand the principle of God's justifying grace can be derived from scripture and on the other demythologising removes from scripture those concepts within it which appear to clash with modern science and philosophy. The yardstick is then both internal and external. In both aspects there is some element of subjectivity. There are Christians who have wrestled with the problems of science and philosophy and have been able to live with their scientific and philosophical friends but have not adopted an existentialist philosophical position; there are also Christians who have not found the centre of their faith in a Pauline doctrine of justification. But if there is an element of subjectivity does this then mean that the individual Christian is in the end his own canonical authority? It is true that the individual in his individual judgment can say 'this is the centre for me' but he cannot say quite as easily 'this (naming some other centre) cannot be the centre for you,' i.e., for some other Christian.

No matter where we look there are problems and it may therefore be simpler at this stage to cut our losses and simply dispense with the concept of a canon. But before we finally accept a solution which involves its ultimate abandonment we ought to look briefly at some of the reasons which have led some to accept the particular canon we have. In doing so we can safely set aside all 'psychological' reasons, i.e., those which

---

[1] We have already seen the difficulty of formulating such a kerygma in invariant terms.

argue that the church must have written authority[1] if it is to
fulfil its tasks or which argue that man as sinful needs something to tell him what is true. Such arguments, even if true, do
not assist us in determining what the canon is. If an authority
of this type is needed other possibilities have been suggested,
e.g., the historic creeds, the ministry of the church or a portion
of it. Of the views which have been advanced some 'absolutize'
the canon, i.e., they defend its necessity on absolute theological
grounds rather than on relative grounds; examples will make
the distinction clear.

(a) A traditional Protestant answer has been that the scriptures are the infallible Word of God and therefore they occupy
a unique position unlike that of any other Christian literature.
This view has always been held in conjunction with others
since by itself it fails to identify which writings are the
scriptures held to be infallible. We therefore move on from it.

(b) If we abandon a view which depends ultimately on a
doctrine of infallible inspiration we might argue that while
much Christian writing is inspired the scriptures are inspired
to a higher degree.[2] This again leaves unresolved the question
how we know which are the scriptures which are inspired and

---

[1] It may be that the term 'authority' used in relation to scripture is less helpful now than in
the past. Protestant apologists originally used it in relation to their controversies with Rome,
arguing for the authority of scripture over against that of the church. Today the discussion of
the place of scripture is conducted instead over against the difficulties which arise out of its
scholarly use and over against a situation in society in the West which is largely without any
clear authority. It is not a question of a clash of 'authorities' but of the nature of the authority
belonging to scripture. Despite the claims of right-wing fundamentalists, especially in the
U.S.A., few Christians deny some measure of authority to scripture; they should take care not
to be lured on to false ground by their opponents through a wrong statement of the question
and an appeal to traditional Protestant faith. It would help the discussion if it were cast in terms
other than those of authority. In setting scripture over against church the Reformers and their
followers did not explore the nature of the authority which adheres to scripture; it was
sufficient for them to reject the authority of the church. It is the nature of this authority that
requires to be discussed today.

[2] Cf. R. Murray, 'How did the Church determine the Canon of Scripture?', *Heythrop
Journal*, xi (1970), 115-26.

that to a higher degree. The writers of the New Testament rarely refer to themselves as inspired whereas the post-canonical writers of the second century quite regularly attribute inspiration to themselves.[1]

(c) Some would say that at some point the church made a decision and that thereby it determined for all time which books are the Word of God, are inspired or belong to the canon. It is difficult to identify the particular point in time at which this decision was made. Some argue for the second century[2] in respect of books which are not disputed;[3] others, more recently, place the point of decision in the fourth century.[4] The decision, of course, need not have been made at any particular point in time but may have been part of a process. Whether, however, we pick on a period of time or a particular date it appears to absolutise this period or date and to absolutise the church as it made its decision. Such a point of view will clearly accord with a doctrine of infallible inspiration in that it is an infallible decision as to what is inspired. It does not, however, harmonise easily with a view which sees scripture as in some way contextual. If we take scripture to belong to and be influenced by its own period then the decision of the church about it will belong to and have been influenced by its own period. We could conclude that a decision of the fourth century was a decision for the church of the fourth century in the light of the situation in which the church existed at that time, but why should that decision be of absolute validity for all time? In particular if we adopt the view of scripture which has been put forward in this paper then a

[1]Cf. A. C. Sundberg, Jr., 'The Bible Canon and the Christian Doctrine of Inspiration', *Interpretation*, xxix (1975), 352-71, who bases his conclusions on the Harvard thesis of E. R. Kalin, 'Argument from Inspiration in the Canonization of the New Testament' (1967).
[2]See O. Cullmann, 'Scripture and Tradition', *S.J.T.*, vi (1953), 113-35.
[3]The 'disputed' books are Hebrews, James, 2 Peter, 2 and 3 John, Jude, Revelation.
[4]Sundberg, art. cit.

decision within the fourth century represents a freezing in the fourth century at that point, but it cannot claim an absolute position as over against other freezings of the tradition at other points. The need for the church to contend against particular heresies may have led it previously to filter out some writings and stress others so that its eventual choice was restricted. But the problems, heresies and needs of later centuries probably will be different. We can safely leave aside all the interesting theological questions which arise from an absolutisation of the action of the Spirit in the fourth century. Is this to be regarded as a part of salvation history or is it that which says what is salvation history? When Cullmann used this argument he could think of the decision as being made in the second century and this was not very far away from what he would have taken to be the period of salvation history, but if the decision was not really taken until the fourth century, as Sundberg would argue, then this is very much out on its own, away from the period of scripture.

(d) Following what they thought Calvin said[1] many Protestants have argued for the self-authenticating nature of scripture.[2] The scriptures present themselves as being spoken by God; if we or the church as a whole are unbiased all we can do is to acknowledge that the word of God is to be found in the scriptures; we are forced to do them homage. The Spirit in our hearts agrees with the Spirit which spoke through the writers. Our conviction of the truth of scripture is derived not from ourselves, nor from a decision of the church, but from a source higher than human conjecture, namely the secret testimony of the Spirit in the heart of the believer. It does appear to be true that people are 'turned on' (self-authentication) by portions of

---

[1] Cf. *Institutes*, 1.7.2, 4; 1.8.1.

[2] This may not be a correct interpretation of Calvin since he argued for authentication through the Spirit, but it represents a commonly held view of what he meant.

scripture; but different people are turned on by different portions and some people are turned on as much by other Christian writings as by scripture itself. The problem created by the differences and/or contradictions of scripture is relevant here; the picture of Paul given in Acts and that provided by his own letters cannot simply and equally authenticate themselves. The Epistle of James did not authenticate itself to Luther. Equally important is the fact that every reader belongs to a context and whatever speaks to him in that context, whatever authenticates itself to him, must be relevant to that context; it must speak to him in that context. Different portions of the scripture may authenticate themselves to a particular believer at different times in his life and those which at one time spoke most clearly may later say little. All this means that unless there is some voice which as a whole authenticates the entire canon the fact that portions of it authenticate themselves to individual Christians or even to groups of Christians cannot give the canon as a whole an absolute position.

There is one view which lies somewhere between the absolute conception and those which are more truly relative. If we adopt the position that knowledge of the historical Jesus is essential to Christian faith, then we require information about him. Only the four Gospels can give us reliable information, even though it may be slender in extent and very difficult to evaluate; apart from them we have almost nothing to help us in reconstructing the historical Jesus. On such a view the four Gospels might then be held to be essential to the canon. But also on such a view there would appear to be no grounds for retaining Paul, Peter or Hebrews since they have nothing to tell us about the historical Jesus which we could not learn from the Gospels. This view would therefore result in a much reduced canon. There are probably few people who would adhere to it in the simple form in which it has been expressed here, though there have been those who held that all subsequent writing, even that of Paul and Peter, distorted the true picture of Jesus and intervened to prevent men from having a true knowledge of him.

Let us now look at some of the 'relative' views.

(*a*) We determine what belongs to the canon by deciding what is apostolic, early and in accordance with the rule of faith. Logically these three tests ought to be examined separately, but they so interpenetrate that it is easier to take them together. Our views today of which writings are apostolic differ considerably from those of the early church, not merely because we would say that the Gospels were not written by apostles, but because even our understanding of the word 'apostle' is different. Therefore the argument is usually put in terms of earliness rather than strict apostolicity. Harmonisation with the rule of faith raises other questions. If Luther had been alive at the time when these decisions about the canon were made he would hardly have agreed that James coheres with the rule of faith as he understood it. The principle of justifying grace was not an explicit part of the rule of faith and was not used by those who framed the canon as a means of distinguishing between the different possible writings.[1] Paul, indeed, suffered a considerable decline during the latter part of the first century and the first part of the second.[2] In fact harmonisation with the rule of faith really means that writings were chosen which agreed with what Christians believed to be important for their faith from the second to the fourth century. But gradually what they believed was itself formed more and more by the writings that existed and which they already thought to be important; the greater the passage of time the more they were centred on

---

[1] It is fascinating to contrast the commentaries of Chrysostom and Luther on Galatians, and see how differently they lay the emphasis.

[2] Cf. W. Bauer, *Orthodoxy and Heresy in Earliest Christianity* (E. T., London, 1972) p. 225; T. F. Torrance, *The Doctrine of Grace in the Apostolic Fathers* (Edinburgh, 1948).

the already accepted writings; the rule of faith was no longer a separate item, but was itself being continuously modified by the earliest of the New Testament writings to receive general acceptance. So in the end harmonisation with the rule of faith became harmonisation with what were the core writings of scripture and the centre of the faith as it was understood to lie in them; the core was established and others were accepted in so far as they could be reconciled with it.[1] The test of earliness would probably be used differently today from the way it was applied in the early church; we have doubts about 2 Peter and the Pastoral Epistles and, interestingly, when we classify a book as late we unconsciously tend to think less of it; its appeal seems to depend upon its age. If, however, earliness is to be the criterion then the decision as to the canon lies in the hands of academics and we are saying in effect that the best sources for our knowledge of the early Christianity are the most suitable books for the canon. We hand ourselves over from the bishops to the scholars and, Presbyterian as I am, if I had to choose I would prefer the bishops. There is a hidden assumption often underlying this approach; what is early is reliable. In some ways this is true; the second-century gospels are much less reliable in the facts they provide about Jesus than those we have from the first century, but Christianity is not just a matter of certain facts; there is the understanding of these facts. Is it true that first understandings are superior to later understandings? If I

---

[1]With the passage of time Christian writers drew increasingly on the existing New Testament writings. The Didache, unlike most of the other writings of the post-apostolic period, hardly quotes the New Testament. A living oral tradition continued into the early second century and the Didache drew from this. This oral traditional naturally died quickly once normative writings were acknowledged. However, some elements outside the New Testament must have entered the streams of tradition and continued to affect Christian belief and practice ever since. A strict New Testament canon would exclude these, yet some of them will have represented important freezings of true tradition proceeding from the centre. Such a view, however, should not be extended to permit a gnostic idea of a secret tradition emanating from the apostles and continuing to exist for a long period.

go to a football match my immediate reactions to occasions when the referee blows up play or allows it to continue are often violent but are, I hope, considerably modified and purified on reflection. Why should the understanding of Christian faith which we find in Paul be assumed to be superior to that which we find in Anselm or Bultmann? To answer that the interpretation of Anselm or Bultmann depends upon the interpretation which is found in Paul is not wholly satisfactory for, while depending on Paul, Anselm and Bultmann may have seen more deeply than Paul. The understanding of life which we find in Shakespeare is almost always more profound than that in the chronicles which he used as sources for many of his plots.[1] Earliness, apostolicity and rule of faith are thus difficult criteria to apply and even if they can be applied they only give us a relative solution for it might again be generally accepted by scholars that 2 Peter was written by Peter or they might conclude that the Didache was written in A.D. 50 by a committee of the apostles appointed by James.

(b) It may be argued that the church sometime during the second century sorted out a hard core of books to which others adhere more or less firmly, a canon with soft edges.[2] This hard core is, in effect, the canon. This is really another form of the argument for earliness but leaves out the books about which today there would be disputes as to their early date and concentrates on those which are undoubtedly from the first century. Apart from this it appears to be open to all the

---

[1] Cf. J. H. Newman, *An Essay on the Development of Christian Doctrine* (London, 1974), p. 100: 'It is indeed sometimes said that the stream is clearest near the spring. Whatever use may fairly be made of this image, it does not apply to the history of a philosophy or sect, which, on the contrary, is more equable, and purer, and stronger, when its bed has become deep, and broad, and full.'

[2] Sundberg, op. cit. p. 364, contests the existence of a core New Testament by the end of the second century.

objections which can be made to the argument from earliness. It means that the existing canon is approximately, but not exactly, correct.

(c) It can be argued that the existence of the canon, a set of writings coming from the first and early second centuries, serves to assure us that we have continuity with the original Christian church,[1] and that our faith is the same as that of the primitive church. This, however, does not free us from all the difficulties which arise from differences and/or contradictions; Luther did not wish to be thought to be in continuity with James![2]

There are difficulties then with all the arguments which isolate certain books as uniquely 'sacred'. No one has come up with a satisfactory solution as to how we determine which books should be in the canon. It may be it is the concept of canon which does not marry easily with a modern view of scripture, and the way in which scripture is now used. Yet the books of the New Testament seem essential to any visible and valid understanding of the Christian faith. What, then, can we say about the place of these books? As we look again at this question we recognise that scripture does not exist in and for

---

[1] Cf. Barth, *Church Dogmatics*, I. 2 (E.T., Edinburgh, 1956), p. 597. Barth's position is, of course, much more deeply argued than is suggested by this one point.

[2] The extension of one particular line of thought in the New Testament can lead to heresy; Marcion extended Paul without 'correction' from the rest of the New Testament. The multiplicity of views in the New Testament helps to preserve from error. The development of a particular freezing may so extend what lies in it that the centre is lost. What is needed in a theological statement or theology today is not the evolution of a New Testament idea or ideas, but the response to that to which the New Testament is itself a set of responses. The New Testament, let alone a particular writing in it, is not the germ from which new theologies steadily grow so that a present theology is the slow unfolding of what lay secretly present from the beginning. Each theology ought to be the freezing in a new culture and set of situations of that which was once frozen in a number of different ways in the New Testament. It may be that the historian can trace the ancestry of modern theology through centuries, but at times there are also radical breaks; when we move sideways these breaks become more obvious; a true Indian christology need have no continuity with a Nicene, but it will have continuity with Jesus Christ through the New Testament.

itself but as a means, and not necessarily the only means, for the church to seek God's will. Since it is impossible to read off from it in any simple way God's will, how can its retention and use be defended?

(1) The books of the New Testament are early. Many published reviews of biographies run along the line: 'the author did not know his subject; I knew him personally'. With the present New Testament writings it can be reasonably held that we can make some form of continuity argument back to Jesus himself; there is no disjunction between the faith that is found in these writings and the faith of Jesus. If, then, our faith can be related to these writings, we can maintain that we stand in continuity with Jesus.

(2) If the argument, however, is made from earliness ought we not to go behind the existing writings to those portions of pre-written tradition which we may discover within them?[1] If, however, it is difficult at times to be precisely sure what these portions are, it is even more difficult to be sure of their original context so that we can see them in the meaning which they possessed for their creators rather than for those like Paul who made use of them. So far as the words of scripture go we can at least be reasonably certain that in all material respects we have the autographs.

(3) At least the earlier portions of the New Testament writings were written while the impact of the life of Jesus was still being felt; as time went by the impact must have lessened. This seems to be a reformulation of the argument that the scriptures were written by apostles or apostolic men, i.e., those who had been in direct or indirect contact with Jesus. It may be a subjective judgment but few feel in the same way the impact of Jesus when they turn to the writings of the second century, especially the apocryphal gospels.

[1] So S. M. Ogden, 'The Authority of Scripture for Theology,' *Interpretation*, xxx (1976), 242-61.

(4) Every understanding of Jesus takes place within a context; the contexts are continually changing with changing culture. To take an absurd example; if we were to choose as normative an interpretation from twentieth-century industrial civilisation we should be using a context which is very different from that of Palestine, or even Rome, in the first century. In order to produce an understanding of Jesus within our twentieth-century industrial culture we have to make a great transformation of context. If, however, we go to the first century some of what we read still stands within its original Palestian culture and almost all the remainder has suffered only one transformation, into a Hellenistic culture. Every transformation from one culture to another is liable to corrupt what is being transformed; the dangers of corruption are least where there are fewest transformations.

(5) It is for this reason that, though later understandings may seem to be more profound, and we cannot deny this possibility while we believe the Spirit guides the church and is still active in it, yet we must prefer the earlier understanding. Later understandings are necessary because every understanding is related to a context; our context is not the same as that of the first-century church.[1] We have through the history of the church a succession of understandings; each of these represents a freezing of the tradition in a particular situation and context. It is in this way that we can look at the creeds of the fourth and fifth centuries, the writings of Thomas Aquinas, Luther or Calvin, the revival of Wesley and the many modern

---

[1] It is precisely here that the idea of profundity of later developments may be challenged. Nicene christology may seem more profound than Pauline but each was written to its own situation; Nicene christology would not have been understood in first-century Rome. No universal claim can be made for later theologies as more profound than earlier; they simply meet their situations better. There is an added difficulty in making judgments about profundity; we who judge are yet again in a different situation from both Paul and the Nicene theologians; we cannot make an absolute and eternally true judgment, only one out of and in relation to our own context.

dynamic christological interpretations. Each later interpretation depends on, though in varying degrees, all the earlier
interpretations; thus it is important to retain the earliest as the
correction to the later. Without the existence of earlier interpretation to act as corrections on those which follow there is a
danger of a continuous deviation from a true or original
understanding into a later false one; this can take place
imperceptibly.

This brings us to the crucial question of norm, since the
canon is often considered to exist principally to determine the
truth of disputed points of doctrine. The true or absolute norm
is Christ or the Word of God or God Himself. I leave this
deliberately undefined for any attempt to define it will be
culturally determined.[1] Any 'freezing' can only be a relative
norm. A relative norm is tied to its context and if we change the
context then it is less effective as a norm. The God whose word
is spoken through the scriptures has to be brought from their
context into our context so that he may speak to us and be our
norm. A parallel can be introduced here. Some at least of the
ethical teaching of the New Testament cannot be directly
applied to our situation. We believe 'You shall love your
neighbour as yourself' still remains true, and we believe that,
given that command, our knowledge of the love of God for us
and the illustrations we have of love in practice in New
Testament contexts, we have the guidance we need so that we
can apply the love commandment in our own situations. Can

---

[1]Cf. p. 228, n. 3. We can either set down an 'essence' whose form changes in response to
situation, nor isolate a permanent element which is invariant while there is another element
which is modified with changing context. This difficulty cannot be solved by speaking of
'substance' and 'accidents', for whatever way we attempt to formulate the absolute norm or
centre it always involves a historical element; the 'Jesus' of Jesus Christ can never be
eliminated. If we want a parallel we should probably look for it in the continuity of personality
within a person. At fifty the person is the same as at five yet very different; at the same age
different aspects appear in differing circumstances. There is always change and yet continuity.
The person is always presenting himself to others in new ways.

we not do the same with God in Christ as the true norm from whom we start and with the scriptures as an illustration of what that norm meant in certain particular contexts? The ethical section of the ten commandments forms a first approximation to the way we may live our personal lives with their particular ethical problems, but it is not a set of absolute rules. We allow for modification. May we not view the New Testament in a similar way as a first approximation? On particular issues people continually ask the church for guidance. This implies that the existing norm (scripture) is not clear; the statements which the churches produce we recognise as useful and applicable for a limited time and in a limited situation. Is this not a useful process in which new partial norms are continually being created, or rather the norm, God through Jesus, is being continually applied to new situations? In applying that norm we are never set free from the scriptures; there is no point at which we can lay them aside and say that they are of no help; but as well as the scriptures there is guidance to be had from all subsequent freezings of the tradition, which themselves depend on what lay earlier right back to the scriptures and the oral teaching which preceded them.

(6) Christianity is not just a theory or a philosophy of life; at its centre lie certain events in history and whether we can delineate these events accurately or not we cannot deny their existence. Thus material which comes from near the events must have an importance which does not belong to material which comes from a later period.

(7) The New Testament contains a variety of interpretations from a variety of contexts. That we cannot unearth a primitive gospel or kerygma is not necessarily a disaster; it may be an advantage. Because our context is very different from that of the first century and because we have to extrapolate from the interpretations of the first century to that which is relevant to ours, it is extremely important that we do not possess only one

interpretation from the first century. The variety of the original context and interpretations allows us to move more easily
to fresh contexts, to make the necessary 'transformations'
between the contexts of the first century and our century. The
Gospel of Luke and the Pastoral Epistles with their non-
existentialist interpretation clearly met a need of the late first
century and the beginning of the second and it can be argued
that they have met the need of many Christians since then.
They have sustained the church through many difficulties and
have enabled it to take care of itself not only in time of
persecution but also in time of heresy. Had we only the
existentialist interpretation of Paul and John, supposing that
their interpretations are purely existentialist, the church might
well have lacked an essential element for its continued existence.

How far can we allow variety to go?[1] Can we admit into our
group of writings a writing which is heretical? But every
writing contains some error or heresy and so it becomes a
question of degree. It may, however, be that the question we
are asking is itself making an assumption we ought to reject, for

[1]It is often argued that while the New Testament contains variety it also sets a limit to the
extent of the permissible variety. If the New Testament is a set of freezings of the tradition
within certain situations and cultures, it is difficult to exclude in advance freezings which
might be different because they arose in different situations and cultures. To insist that any
christology emerging in Indian culture should fall within the limits of the varieties of the New
Testament would lead to an almost impossible situation: how can the terms of Indian culture
and philosophy be equated with those of Greek or Jewish culture and philosophy? (Cf. L.
Newbigin, 'Christ and the Cultures', *S.J.T.*, xxxi (1978), 1-22). The first Christians did not
allow the varieties of christology existing within Jewish Christianity to limit those which
appeared in Helenistic Christianity solely on the grounds that they had not been present in
Jewish Christianity. What we can ask of an Indian christology is that it point to the same centre
as do the christologies of the New Testament. If the true canon is not a set of writings, but
God through Jesus Christ, this difficulty can be avoided. We should note that in practice the
Church, in particular the early Church, has tended to move by defining what is unacceptable
rather than what is acceptable. Dunn, op. cit. p. 383, speaks of the New Testament as 'the
initial statement (complex in itself) of the theme on which all that follows are but variations'.
I would prefer to regard the New Testament as the first extant set of variations on the theme,
the theme being God in Christ — the final phrase 'God in Christ' is only a symbol for the
undefinable centre.

it only becomes a real question if we wish to select a 'core' of documents to act as an absolute norm. If we reject this the question appears in a new light. Many will testify that they have learned something of their Christian faith, not only from the New Testament, from Christians writers and teachers, but also from some of those who deliberately reject Christianity, e.g., Nietzsche, Sartre; Jewish scholars are also often quoted appreciatively in Christian writings. It is as if the light who is Jesus shines most clearly in certain writings, the scriptures, less clearly in others, e.g., Thomas, Luther, and just a little in many others. The further we move from the centre the less light there is. The presence of the 'centre' may be relatively slight in some writings but it is not necessarily absent. The writings where it is most clearly seen are the writings which are the most useful. Thus to exclude James from the core would be to deny that James has often been of great benefit to Christians.[1]

(8) These writings of the New Testament can be said to have demonstrated their power to sustain the life of the church through many centuries and so their continued use is not a private or subjective judgment. It proceeds not only from the individual Christian consciousness, the decision of scholars and the decrees of bishops, but also from the continued life of the church. But that does not mean that we should accord to each of these writings the same validity and importance and should ignore other Christian writings of the second and perhaps the first centuries. These also because of their interpretations and their varied contexts can help us to reach the true interpretations in our context. Indeed when we wish to discover the interpretation for our context we may need to use all the interpretations of church history. There is an essential continuity throughout the history of the church and the freezings of tradition in its major points between us and Jesus. The freezings which we call

---

[1]Kosuke Koyama, *Water Buffalo Theology* (London, 1974), pp. 161-9, shows how in some situations in the younger churches James has great value.

the New Testament are just the most useful of these. If we need them, we also need the later freezings.

All this means that it would be wrong to speak of a closed canon as if there was some set number of books. It would also be wrong to speak of certain creeds from the fourth and fifth centuries of the church as possessing an absolute position. Perhaps what the United Presbyterian Church of the U.S.A. has done in binding together the creeds and the reformed confessions and looking upon the whole as the document which should guide it in its present interpretation suggests a more satisfactory solution. We have much to learn for our own understanding of God's will for us from the period which lies between the New Testament and ourselves and many people will testify that they have been brought to a deeper understanding of Christ not directly by use of the scriptures but by those who have interpreted them in their own generation. In a sense every interpretation goes back through scripture to God through Jesus but the interpretation which speaks to me may not come directly from scripture but be mediated through the church or some teacher within the church. But then again what precedes, and especially the New Testament, stands as a protection to preserve that which follows from erroneous interpretation.

To conclude: it is better to speak of the New Testament as primary: primary because it is the first of the long series of responses by Christians expressing their faith and what they understood to be God's will in definite situations, and primary because every succeeding response depends on it. The formulation of a response to God in our situation would be impossible today without every preceding interpretation; that was also true of every earlier age and its interpretation; if we work back in this way we eventually come to the New Testament itself; all that follows it goes back to it.[1] There is nothing earlier

[1]Should a lost letter of Paul be discovered we can imagine the difficulty the churches would be in; it might, for instance, be argued that the canon was settled by the undivided church and

than scripture on which we can depend and everything after depends on it. In that sense it is essential as well as primary. Every understanding of God through Christ is funnelled back through scripture to God and then forward again to us.

that no action should be taken to include the new letter into the canon until the church was again one. The understanding of scripture suggested above is more flexible and would allow the use of such a newly discovered letter.

2

INTERPRETING THE NEW TESTAMENT AND INTERPRETING CHRIST

The angle from which we approach any document and the presuppositions with which we come clearly affect the way we interpret it. A historian of music comes to a Beethoven sonata with different questions in mind from those of a concert pianist. I approach Scripture as an academic who is paid to interpret it and as a Christian who holds the NT in high regard. I do not approach it as one who accepts its verbal infallibility. Clearly this leaves open a considerable number of options.

Let me begin with a simple question: From time to time church drama groups present biblical plays: should the characters be dressed in biblical or in modern costume? In either case a theological position is implied. If the characters are dressed as in the first century, the remoteness of what is said in the play becomes apparent; if the characters are dressed in the clothes we wear the historical nature of Christianity is lost. The issues will become more clear as we continue. As a first step we need to realise that this is a modern problem. If you look at paintings of biblical scenes made at any time prior to the nineteenth century you will see that the characters are dressed in the clothes of the artist's own day and the scenery is that of the artist's own country, usually Italian or Dutch. However in some of the paintings of the pre-Raphaelites (as those by Hunt, Millais) the characters wear clothing drawn from the biblical period and depicted with great accuracy. Painters prior to the nineteenth century did not think about the matter; they saw no problem. The pre-Raphaelites saw a problem and solved it in one particular way. How and why did this change come about? This is a very simple statement of one of the underlying problems in biblical interpretation and before we are finished we shall see that we have to qualify it in many ways.

The Reformers by the very nature of the appeal to the authority of Scripture were forced to evolve a theory of the interpretation of Scripture. Previously it had been held that Scripture could be interpreted in more than one way, allegorisation being particularly important, though as we approach the time of the Reformation we find that the literal sense is gradually gaining the upper hand and interpretation is expected to accord with that sense. Both Luther and Calvin strongly affirm that the only valid sense of Scripture was the literal. In practice Luther did not always adhere as closely to this sense as Calvin. Not only was the Gospel clear in its essential sense to any one who read Scripture, but most of the Scripture itself in its literal sense would be clear to anyone. Those parts which were not at once clear could be clarified in respect of their meaning from other passages that were clear. Scripture being clear in this way could be applied directly to the lives of men or, if some adjustments had to be made, these were perfectly obvious. Thus Luther, while applying the arguments of Paul in Galatians to personal salvation and the lives of believers, also adapted much of what Paul said against the Judaizers into attacks on the Pope and his followers. To Luther this seemed to be a simple and clear updating of the literal sense of Scripture for his own situation.

By and large the Reformers and their successors found it easy to apply most of Scripture directly to their own situations. The world of the sixteenth century was very like that of the first century: people thought and behaved in the same way; personal salvation could be conceived in the same way; ethical problems had hardly changed. If we go back to our original question, the answer of the Reformers would have been: put Jesus in dress contemporary with yourself; it makes no difference.

The search for the literal sense of Scripture once begun led finally to the historical-critical movement, the modern way of interpreting Scripture. The process was long and devious and many outside influences played a part in it. We cannot examine these in detail. There was the discovery of the New World and the realisation that the world's centre did not lie in Jerusalem or Judaea; this was symbolised by the selection of Greenwich as zero longitude. A civilisation as old as that of Israel, but with a chronology different from Israel's, was discovered in Egypt. Descartes sent modern philosophy on its way by taking as his starting-point not God but himself. The scientific movement asserted that proof lay in examination and observation rather than in the acceptance of authority. Within the church the literal sense came to be understood as closely associated with the intention of the writer. Despite the assertion that Scripture was its own interpreter and ought to be interpreted from within itself it was soon realised that there were passages which could not be understood without passing beyond the bounds of Scripture. The Greek and Latin Classics were searched for parallels to words and thoughts; the Jewish writings were re-read for the light they could throw upon the Jewish authors of the NT and the life and time of Jesus. Thus the minds of the original writers were illuminated with material drawn from outside Scripture and so illuminated were better understood.

Though historians existed in the Greek and Roman world and though chroniclers and historians continued to be found from time to time in the Middle Ages and afterwards there was no serious study of history as such. Whenever it was studied or written about this was done in order either to glorify the past of a particular dynasty or to give guidance to the present; it was never studied purely as an interest in itself. History was not included in the curriculum of the ancient world from which those of the Middle Ages and the post-Reformation period were derived; only in the nineteenth century for the first time were history and archaeology studied seriously; it was 1893 before a Chair of History was founded in the University of Glasgow, and Glasgow was not particularly late in this. The discoveries archaeologists brought back from Greece and the Middle East to European centres of culture showed quickly and clearly that people had dressed very differently in the ancient world both from what the sixteenth and later centuries believed and from what was worn in the nineteenth century. This combined with the emphasis of the historians on the correct reporting of historical facts quickly led in the visual arts to the presentation of first century characters in first century dress. Hence the stress some artists began to lay on depicting characters drawn from the NT in first century garb.

Before we go on we should note one important feature of the historical method, a feature which would have been rejected by the successors to the Reformers. When we attempt to discover what was in the mind of its original writers, the literal sense of Scripture, we have to treat Scripture as we would treat any other writing. Scripture cannot be given a special status, nor can any section of it be exempt from the same examination as the same event or narrative would receive if the account of it was found in another book. The literal sense must be the sense detected by the ordinary methods of historical analysis. In the nineteenth century it was assumed that the application of these methods to historical material would result in highly probable, if not certain, results in respect of events in the past. Historians expected that just as physical scientists could produce conclusions which would be accepted by anyone who examined their experiments, so they, the historians, could produce equally sure conclusions about the past, which anyone who examined the evidence would accept. Returning to our initial question about the presentation of Jesus in a biblical play that would mean that if we were to present a biblical play showing Jesus in first century guise, then we could do this without any dispute as to the way in which he was portrayed. Unfortunately for such a view historians today are much less confident of our ability to create a picture of the past which would be generally accepted. They realise that when they examine the evidence from the past, estimate its reliability and the relationship of one piece of evidence to another, they allow their modern presuppositions to govern the way in which they view the evidence. Thus the hoped for neutral picture of Jesus in first century guise will be in part shaped in terms of today. We have certain views about the development and understanding of personality; these views may have a Freudian or Jungian slant and the slant will force us to look at Jesus from that particular angle and may lead us to explain him in terms drawn from a modern psychological theory. The modern view of an incident in the life of Jesus or of the development of his character would then be incomprehensible to a person from the first century, even if we could be assured that it would accurately represent what happened then.

This means that one side of the original two alternatives must be qualified. We are unable to present Jesus or any figure from the biblical period in a natural and unambiguous way so that he fits into that period and is at the same time able to be understood by us. If we are to understand we need to be able to present the ancient world in terms that belong to our world. We shall later go on to examine the other alternative and find that it also needs to be qualified; however we can see now how our initial question arose. Interest in history together with a rapidly changing modern world made men realise the great difference between the world of the first century and our world. It was no longer possible to evade the problem simply by dressing Jesus in contemporary clothing knowing that no one would perceive the difference. Today with the spread of education everybody sees the difference.

As we have looked at the problem we shall have begun to realise that it is not simply the question of the dress that Jesus or any first century figure wore that makes the difference between the first century and this century, nor is it such a simple thing as the change in transport from chariot to car. The problem facing the artist who attempts to represent a biblical scene is comparatively simple. The problem facing the man or woman who wishes to interpret the Bible for today is much more profound and complex. One aspect of this can be illustrated by a re-telling of the story of the Samaritan.

> A man was going down from Jerusalem to Jericho, and fell among robbers, who stripped him and beat him, and departed, leaving him half-dead. Now by chance a priest was going down that road and when he saw him he passed by on the other side. So likewise a Levite, when he came to the place and saw him, passed by on the other side. A Samaritan came along and saw the man lying at the side of the road. He went across and realised that he was a Jew. At that moment the man opened his eyes, looked up and whispered "Help me". The Samaritan kicked him in the teeth. Then when he saw that, although he was almost naked, he had on a decent pair of trousers, he undid the zip, pulled them off, rolled the man to the edge of the road and pushed him over the cliff. Taking the trousers he went on to the next village. In the inn there he sold them for two pence.

That is how every Jew expected the story to end when Jesus began it. Jesus' conclusion was as sharp a kick in the teeth to his Jewish hearers as the Samaritan had given the injured man. None of us can today experience the gut reaction that Jesus' hearers had when they heard the story as Jesus told it. We miss that gut reaction because the story is so familiar, but even more so because in most parts of the Western world there is no radical division within society in which one portion of it hates the other with the venom with which Jew and Samaritan hated each other. Making the priest into a bishop, the Levite into an elder and the Samaritan into a commercial traveller, as I have heard done, will not bring the story alive in the way it was alive in Palestine in the first century. The difference between our society and that of the first century Palestine is not one of dress alone, but the absence of a deep cleft which ran through Jewish society. Undoubtedly there are many little clefts in Western society but that is not the same. Northern Ireland is the only country in western society in which there is such a deep division as existed in Palestine in the first century. There, at least, the story ought to be understood.

A word needs to be said about the familiarity of biblical stories and therefore the difficulty of understanding them. During the centuries as music has developed it has experienced many innovations. At the time they were recognised as new, and those who heard them objected strongly. Today we hear the same music but any idea of its 'newness' has gone. Our ears are attuned to accept what seemed strange to the music's first hearers. Our ears equally miss the newness in stories from the NT. Like the music the stories have become part of our culture.

We need then to look at the differences between our society and that of the Bible. Of course man is basically the same kind of being now as he was then, a mixture of goodness and selfishness. Many individual problems within the field of the family and personal relationships still exist in the same intensity as they possessed in the first century; on the other hand, as we shall see, new problems have appeared and some old ones have disappeared or no longer worry us. Man is still called on to deny himself, to take up his cross and to lose his life for the sake of Christ and the Gospel, though the way in which he does these may be different today from the time of the Bible.

It is undoubtedly true that on the one hand life seems to have shrunk, the borders of the world are so much closer; on the other hand life has become very much more complex. Until a few generations ago most people lived their entire lives within the village or small town in which they had been born; they rarely moved out of its area. Occasionally a war might recruit them, but even then they did not go far afield often; they remained to fight for their own area. The wealthy may have made the 'grand tour' but they were only a tiny few. Contrast that with the way in which people move around today; almost any one can, in fact many do, go overseas for their holidays. The world has shrunk, and shrinking it has become more complex. Fifty years ago it did not matter how what would then have been thought of as minor Arab rulers acted; today we take an avid interest in what they do. The industrialisation of Japan closes motor factories in Britain. Cheap labour in Hong-Kong brings unemployment to the mills of Lancashire.

Not merely has life shrunk and become more complex but attitudes have vastly changed. If I go out and find my car will not start I look for a mechanic; in the ancient world I would have looked for a magician. If a cow goes dry, the farmer calls in the vet and not the witch doctor. If we want to know what the future holds, we do not kill a bird and examine its entrails or have an astrologer read the stars for us; we send for a statistician to tell us about general trends and we base our decisions upon his conclusions. We no longer attribute what happens to us to the gods or to evil powers. When we want to find out if a fact or a theory is true we do not sit down and argue about it but we observe, experiment and draw conclusions.

If you then want to present Jesus or some other NT character in a play for today how do you go about it? Let me set up a few unfinished scenarios of the way in which this might be attempted.

Jesus was flying back from Dublin to Manchester. In the airport lounge he noticed this woman who was very agitated. By chance he found himself sitting beside her on the plane. She began to talk to him. She told him that she was flying over to Manchester to her sister who had made all the arrangements.

'You see it's my sixth,' she said. 'The last isn't a year old yet and the oldest is only seven. I am just worn down with looking after them and I can't have another'. Finish the story by telling how Jesus advised the woman, and realise that different people will finish it in very different ways.

Paul was travelling up from Sheffield to London by train. He begins to talk to the man in the seat next to him and learns that he is a trade union official going up to a union conference to decide whether to have a strike or not. They are not a large or powerful union and have few resources to fall back on; they had lost out badly in the last round of wage increases; if they had a rise, others would demand that differentials be maintained; there would be inflation all round; because of their weakness they might in any case have to settle for something less than their fair increase. What does Paul say?

It would be quite easy to go on multiplying instances like this. You can see that once you put Jesus or Paul into modern clothing you release a whole set of problems for which there are no easy answers. Yet it is these problems which we often try to solve using the NT. How then are we to interpret the NT?

The problem is intensified because a great deal of what we find in the NT is tied down to its own particular situation. The story of the good Samaritan was a good illustration of this. There are many more. Jesus said that new wine put into old bottles would split them. The obvious reference is to the new faith which Jesus brought as destructive of the old Jewish faith. For the first Christians the relationship of Christianity to Judaism was a live issue; it is not for the vast majority of congregations in almost every part of the world today. We can understand intellectually the change from Judaism to Christianity, but we cannot experience it as an existential problem. A great part of the NT is couched just in terms of this change. Paul's teaching on justification by faith relates to the Jewish law. The teaching of Hebrews on the sacrifice of Jesus is based on the Jewish sacrificial cultus. It is not easy to transfer such passages, and remember they are very large sections of the NT, to our situation and find easy parallels. Do we then just set them entirely aside and pay no heed to them because today it is impossible to apply them directly?

Let me pick up a point which ought perhaps to have been introduced earlier but comes in more easily now. Do we interpret the NT or do we interpret Christ? Without a doubt in the church we are sent to interpret Christ. We do not set out to see which parts of the NT speak with power to our situation, but to see how Christ himself speaks to us within our situation. Once we say this we see new aspects of our problem. So far we have talked mainly about ethical problems and moral situations. The question of Christology ought to have been raised before this. Now it becomes acute.

At Caesarea Philippi Jesus asked his disciples what they and others were saying about him. The disciples reported that people were saying that he was John the baptizer or Elijah or one of the prophets. These are all Jewish terms and are hardly the kind of estimates that any one would make of Jesus today. The disciples for their part confess he is the Christ; this is also a Jewish term. We have become used to it, though we rarely appreciate its meaning. It would have meant nothing to Greeks in the ancient world other than that after a bath they had rubbed oil into their skin to soften it; it had no religious value for them as it had for Jews. The Christians quickly had to begin to express their faith in Jesus, using terms which would be understood both in the Jewish and the Greco-Roman worlds, so they used terms like Son of God or Lord. We know how the discussion went on for centuries and how orthodox christology was forged on the basis of current philosophical concepts and psychological ideas of personality. If we wished to update Caesarea Philippi we would not wish to express the alternatives to 'Christ' in Jewish terms, for these would need to be explained to people if they are to grasp their significance and thus his. With whom then should be contrast Christ and what terms should we use to describe him? There is no christology in fixed terms which we can bring into every situation. The very expression of christology is itself subject to the culture and situation in which it is verbalised.

If we distinguish between interpreting Christ and interpreting the NT we need to say something about the relation of the NT to Christ. The books of the NT might be looked on as a number of windows through which we can look at Christ. The preacher does not preach a particular book of the NT, e.g., he does not preach Mark, but he preaches or interprets Christ as seen through the window of Mark. Another analogy would describe Christ as a theme-tune and the NT as variations on it. We have no access to the original tune except through the variations. To interpret Christ for ourselves is to produce the variation in our situation which is appropriate to that situation and culture. The books of the NT might yet again be regarded as similar to photographs of a great building. No one photograph can include more than one aspect of the building; we must photograph from south or east or north or west; each picture only gives a limited view. It takes all the photographs to begin to build up the total picture. The building is more than each individual picture, even more than all the pictures taken together. And the stance from which we need a photograph today may not be any of the positions from which the original photographs were taken.

None of these metaphors is perfect, and none of the books of the NT gives a perfect representation of Christ. They are tied to their own situation and limited by the peculiarities of that situation and the failings of their writers. It might seem that we could extrapolate from their situation to ours, but any statistician will tell you that to extrapolate from a given set of figures to produce a prediction of what may happen is a very dangerous process. Yet this is what we have to do, given the NT. From it and the personalities, incidents, events, teaching, etc. it provides we have to bring Christ into our situation and our culture. To interpret the NT we have to interpret that which the NT itself interprets, the act of God in Christ.

I do not intend to provide examples of how this may be done. Needless to say when I preach or teach I am concerned with this process of interpretation but here I am concerned only with the theory which underlies the process and I only need to indicate some of the guidelines along which interpretation must always take place.

(1) We need to know as much as we can about what the author meant when he wrote some particular bit of the NT, about the situation of his readers and how they would understand what he wrote, about the ancient world in general and how people thought and acted then. That means that we use the historical-critical method with all the exactitude and rigour that is possible. This knowledge alone does not as we have seen provide an interpretation valid for today of either the NT or Christ, but it is an essential preliminary.

There is a subsidiary point to be made. Within the Christian church subsequent to the writing of Scripture there has been a continual process of re-understanding what God has done in Christ in relation to the changing situation of the church; examining that process we can see how the church's understanding of Christ has changed with changing context. A knowledge of church history is therefore of assistance in helping us to see how we may understand. And it will also be of assistance since we stand in the direct continuous chain of Christian witness which goes back to the first apostles. It is this chain which we wish to extend into our period.

There is however one error that needs to be avoided here, the error of stopping in some period of church history. When sixteenth century painters depicted biblical characters in sixteenth century dress that was perhaps excusable; what was not excusable was eighteenth century painters depicting biblical characters in sixteenth century dress. Too often we are satisfied to depict Christ in terms of the Reformation or the counter-Reformation and to forget that the world has moved on since then.

(2) Whoever would interpret for Christians the scriptural report of God's work in Christ in its relation to today must participate in the Christian experience; he stands at the end of that chain of witness that goes back to the beginning and is a part of it. The agnostic scholar can argue cogently about the meaning of Scripture as it was intended by its authors, and many agnostics and Jewish scholars have contributed greatly in the search after the meaning of the NT within the first century and so brought genuine insights into its meaning. The interpretation for the church today must however come from those who stand within the Christian experience. This experience is never individual but always corporate. The Christian who attempts to interpret draws from an existing experience, that of the whole church, and in turn contributes to it. He depends not only on his contemporaries but also on all the past life of the church. He expresses the individual aspect of this experience by saying that he interprets as one who has the mind of Christ (1 Cor. 2.16), who by the Lord's mercy is trustworthy (1 Cor. 7.35), who has the charisma of the utterance of wisdom and knowledge (1 Cor. 12.8), or who knows the living and exalted Christ.

(3) All interpretation takes place on the basis of a theological and philosophical position. The culture in which we have been brought up, the church tradition in which we have been nurtured and the thought we have given to working out our own theological position determine the way in which we interpret every part of Scripture and in the end interpret Christ. If we go back to the example of the woman flying to

Manchester for an abortion the way in which we would finish the scenario will depend to a very high degree on the philosophical and theological presuppositions we bring to it. If we believe that life begins at conception we shall certainly decide in one way; if we do not hold this belief we may have others which affect us in determining what advice we would give the woman. What we have also to observe is that our cultural, theological and philosophical viewpoints are in part determined by the existing way in which we interpret Christ. As we interpret him in relation to an existing situation so we should in fact be readjusting the philosophical, theological and cultural views with which we started. We must always be ready to allow this to happen, otherwise, in a real sense, the solutions we reach are already dictated for us before we approach Scripture and Christ. And since we cannot interpret in any other way than through theological, philosophical and cultural presuppositions it must be our duty always to re-examine these so that we never make absolute claims for our own interpretations.

(4) It is all very well knowing everything about the original meaning of a passage in Scripture and possessing a true and valuable experience of Christ and of the church and an awareness of the theology and philosophy which determine many of our decisions but all this is useless unless there is added to it a sensitivity to the world in which we live. The context in which we interpret is both universal, we belong to a common culture, and particular, we are dealing with particular situations. Christological re-interpretation will belong to the former; it cannot be over-particularised. Many personal ethical problems belong to a particular situation and a solution to them must be found in relation to that situation. Work at the original meaning of Scripture will show us the difference between the culture of our world and the world as it was two thousand years ago, but there is more to this than just knowing the difference. It is necessary to be aware of the real problems

that affect people today; but to approach the matter through 'problems' is, perhaps, to take the wrong approach; we can learn about the intricacies of making a decision in respect of abortion, unemployment and war but these are not the only issues which affect people. Whoever wishes to interpret must be sensitive to the loneliness and anxieties of one kind or another which affect individuals, sensitive also to the moods of an age, its despair or optimism.

(5) The ultimate interpretation of the NT is not into a new set of words, but into a life lived amongst people. Theologians look for a new formula in words that will express the christology relevant to our culture; moralists look for solutions to the problems with which we are faced in our varying situations; preachers attempt to apply texts to their congregations. All end by using a set of words. The translation that really counts is not that into words but that into lives. The NT is a set of words but as such it is a set of words which leads us back to the activity of God in Christ. The theme tune to which it provides variations is not a verbalised 'idea' but an actual life lived by a real person. The only ultimate translation of this is into another life. Words are one stage on the way from the actual loving existence of Jesus to the re-expression of his love in the lives of man today. The life which is to appear must be a life based on his life and be a true exegesis of it. It must also be part of a community of lives, a part of the body of Christ which itself is an actual re-presentation of the life of Christ. It must be so lived amongst other lives that it is sensitive to their needs and attempts to meet those needs.

3

THE LITERAL MEANING OF SCRIPTURE, THE HISTORICAL CRITICAL METHOD AND THE INTERPRETATION OF SCRIPTURE

Those who prowl around art galleries can notice a significant change between paintings of biblical scenes made in the sixteenth or seventeenth centuries and those made from the middle of the nineteenth century onwards to the end of that century. In the earlier paintings biblical characters wear clothes contemporary with the period of the artist and the background scenery is usually Dutch or Italian. If however you look at the later work of some of the pre-Raphaelites you see that there is an exactness in the dressing of the characters so that they wear the kind of clothes which it is believed were worn in the first century and the background is that of Palestine (Holman Hunt visited Palestine to ensure the accuracy of his backgrounds). There is a similar change in the work of biblical scholars and it takes place at some period between the sixteenth and the end of the nineteenth centuries though, of course, the changes in art and biblical scholarship are not related directly but indirectly.

Problems of interpretation exist from the moment scripture is intellectually examined. Philo pointed in the Old Testament to anthropomorphisms, to impossibilities (from where did Cain get his wife) and to immoralities. To escape these difficulties he allegorised. Christian scholars, in particular Origen, took up where Philo left off. The problem for them was wider in two respects; they had to find Christ in the Old Testament and they had to deal with difficulties in the New Testament. In the latter there are still anthropomorphisms (e.g. the anger of God, Jesus as sitting at God's right hand), impossibilities or contradictions (e.g. how to equate the first few days of Jesus' ministry as depicted in the fourth gospel and in the synoptic gospels[1]), immoralities (e.g. the murder of Ananias and Sapphira, the payment by Jesus of the temple tax through a trick). These difficulties could be avoided by turning attention away from the literal sense of scripture to other meanings, the moral, the allegorical, the anagogic.

Origen seems to take a delight in finding difficulties in the literal sense so that he can ignore it and apply his mind to the spiritual. Scholars gradually came to terms with this. On the one hand the worst excesses of the allegorical method were eliminated and it was confined to the confirmation of truth already accepted within the church. On the other hand it was realised that the literal sense was not the exact meaning of the words but should instead be related to the intention of the writer; consequently metaphor could be recognised as a metaphor because it was so intended by the writer and parables did not need to be taken literally. By the end of the middle ages the literal meaning is being accepted as the most important meaning for the establishment of theological truth.

By the very nature of the controversy[2] which broke out at the time of the Protestant Reformation the reformers were forced to stress the authority of the bible[3] as over against the authority

---

[1]Origen points out the difficulties in great detail (*Comm. Joh.* X, 1-3 (1-14); *G. C. S.* Origen IV, 170-3.

[2]Luther formulated his views most clearly in controversy with Erasmus. For a discussion of the controversy see O. Kuss, 'Über der Klarheit der Schrift. Historische und hermeneutische Überlegungen zu der Kontroverse des Erasmus und des Luther über den freien oder versklavten Willen', in *Schriftauslegung* (ed. J. Ernst), München 1972, 89-149.

[3]This emphasis goes back to Wyclif. M. Deanesly (*The Lollard Bible*) says that Wyclif strove 'Expressly to defend the value of the Bible as the final authority; to show that the people at large were ignorant of the Gospel because of defective preaching; then, that it was necessary for all, even the simplest, to know the Gospel, that they might follow Christ in meekness of living; then, that the Gospels ought to be translated into English, for this end; and finally, that it was right that such translations had been made, though prelates raged against them.' (Quoted in A. Peel, 'The Bible and the People: Protestant Views of the Authority of the Bible', in *The Interpretation of the Bible* (ed. C. W. Dugmore) London 1944, 55).

of the church or of the pope within the church. If the church is to be reformed then there must be a standard according to which the reform is carried out. For Luther scripture provided that standard. Once the authority of scripture is stressed the way in which it is interpreted becomes all important. Two main principles emerged: (1) The most important sense was the literal, clear or simple sense;[4] (2) scripture was its own interpreter. The protestants were forced to stress the literal meaning of scripture because allegorisation could produce meanings out of scripture with which they did not agree. They were forced to stress scripture as its own interpreter because this preserved authority within scripture, eliminating the need for someone, or some body, outside scripture to say what it meant.

Each of these principles could be understood in two ways. It might almost be said that each was ambiguous, an ambiguity which only slowly became apparent, for each expresses both a dogmatic position and a literary rule of interpretation.

Scripture is clear in its literal meaning. In the first or dogmatic sense this means that to the man who has the Spirit of God the way of salvation is expressed openly and simply within scripture and there is no need in order to understand it to be deeply learned or to have the assurance of the church that any particular interpretation is correct. Because of the internal clarity of scripture

> anyone who is enlightened concerning himself and his own salvation, judges and discerns with the greatest certainty the dogmas and opinions of all men.[5]

---

[4]Again cf. Wyclif
'Their meaning was plain even to the simple, and as it was the first duty of the priest to expound them and proclaim the good news they contained, so it was the duty of every believer in lesser degree (Peel, *op. cit.*, 55)'.
[5]*The Bondage of the Will* (ET by P. S. Watson and B. Drewery), Lib. Christ. Classes XVII, 159 = *WA* 18.653; cf. p. 112 = *WA* 18.609.

When men fail to understand the internal clarity of scripture it is not because of the difficulties of the words but because of the hardness of their hearts:

> It is true that for many people much remains abstruse; but this is not due to the obscurity of scripture, but to the blindness or indolence of those who would not take the trouble to look at the very clearest truth.[6]

The internal clarity speaks Christ and what does not speak Christ is not scripture. In this way Luther was moved to criticise even the canon of scripture:

> It is the office of a true apostle to preach the passion and resurrection and work of Christ, and to lay down the true ground for this faith, as Christ himself says in John 15, You shall be my witness. All genuinely sacred books are unanimous here, and all preach Christ emphatically. The true touchstone for testing every book is to discover whether it emphasises the prominence of Christ or not . . . What does not teach Christ is not apostolic, not even if taught by Peter or Paul. On the other hand, what does preach Christ is apostolic, even if Judas, Annas, Pilate, or Herod does it.[7]

Luther therefore refuses the letter of James a place in the canon of scripture.

The second aspect of the clear or literal meaning of scripture relates to its proclamation:

> If . . . you speak of the external clarity, nothing at all is left obscure or ambiguous, but everything there is in the scriptures has been brought out by the Word into the most definite light, and published to all the world.[8]

This is closely linked to the method of interpretation. At many points Luther emphasises the external clarity of the words and the need to accept the literal sense.

> We must everywhere stick to the simple, pure and natural sense of words that accords with the rules of grammar and the normal use of language as God created it in man.[9]

---

[6] *Op. cit.*, 111 = 18.607.
[7] Preface to the Epistles of St James and St Jude (ET as in B. L. Woolf, *Reformation Writings of Martin Luther* II, 307 = *WADB* 7.385.
[8] *Bondage*, 112 = *WA* 18.609.
[9] *Op. cit.*, 221 = *WA* 18.700.

(The Word of God's) plainest meanings are to be preserved; and unless the context manifestly compels one to do otherwise, the words are not to be understood apart from their proper and literal sense, lest occasion be given to our adversaries to evade scripture as a whole.[10]

What God says must be taken quite simply at its face value.[11]

Luther certainly acknowledged that obscure passages existed but he attributed them to our linguistic and grammatical ignorance. All important matters in the scriptures are 'clear, open and evident'.[12] Luther did not of course deny that it is necessary to labour to understand the scriptures. He expected his contemporaries to labour as hard at the word of God as had the fathers of the church.[13]

We conclude with a quotation from Calvin who wrote in his Commentary on Galatians:

With such approbation the licence increased more and more, so that he who played this game of allegorising Scripture not only was suffered to pass unpunished but even obtained the highest applause. For many centuries no man was thought clever who lacked the cunning and daring to transfigure with subtlety the sacred Word of God. This was undoubtedly a trick of Satan to impair the authority of Scripture and remove any true advantage out of the reading of it. God avenged this profanation with a just judgment when He suffered the pure meaning to be buried under false glosses.

Scripture, they say, is fertile and thus bears multiple meanings. I acknowledge that Scripture is the most rich and inexhaustible fount of all wisdom. But I deny that its fertility consists in the various meanings which anyone may fasten to it at his pleasure. Let us know, then, that the true meaning of Scripture is the natural and simple one (*verum sensum scripturae, qui germanus est et simplex*), and let us embrace and hold it resolutely. Let us not merely neglect as doubtful, but boldly set aside as deadly corruptions, those pretended expositions which lead us away from the literal sense (*literali sensu*).[14]

---

[10] *The Pagan Servitude of the Church*, Woolf, I, 226 = *WA* 6.509.

[11] *Bondage*, 223 = *WA* 18.702f. Cf. *Pagan Servitude* 311f. = *WA* 6.562.

[12] *Bondage*, 163 = *WA* 18.656.

[13] *WA* 7.100 (quoted in G. Ebeling, *The Word of God and Tradition*, London 1968, 252).

[14] Ad 4.22 (ET by T. H. L. Parker; Edinburgh 1965) = *CR* 78.

We now look at the second principle. 'Scripture is its own interpreter.' This again can be understood both as a dogmatic principle and as a literary rule of interpretation. In the first case it means that scripture is a closed circle whose ultimate writer is the Holy Spirit; he alone can interpret himself; his words in one part of scripture may be used to interpret difficulties in another part. This takes seriously the nature of scripture as revelation; it is also closely related to Luther's doctrine of Sola Scriptura and as we have seen to his quarrel with Rome, but also to his quarrel with protestant extremists, for these, Luther alleges 'Subject the Scriptures to the interpretation of their own spirit'.[15] Two further quotations will suffice; the first is from Luther and the second from the first Helvetic Confession (1536):

> That it (scripture) may, by itself, be its own interpreter the most certain, the easiest, the most accessible, proving all things, judging and illuminating.[16]

> The interpretation of Holy Scripture is to be sought from it alone, that it may be the interpreter of itself, the rule of faith and love being in the chair.[17]

We can see that what I have termed the dogmatic understanding of the two principles of the literal meaning and of scripture as its own interpreter are closely related in that both depend upon the recognition of the activity of the Holy Spirit in scripture. So Luther can say

> Scripture is to be understood only by that spirit in which scripture was written, because the spirit is never found more present and lively than in the sacred writings themselves.[18]

There is of course implied the non-contradictory nature of scripture:

[15] *Bondage*, 158 = *WA* 18.702; cf. p. 163 = *WA* 18.656.
[16] *WA* 7.97 (quoted in Ebeling, *op. cit.* 248).
[17] See Heppe, *Reformed Dogmatics*, 34.
[18] *WA* 7.97 (quoted in Bainton, *Cambridge History of the Bible*, Vol. III, ed. S. L. Greenslade, 21).

There is no inconsistency in the statements of scripture.[19]

We now turn to the second, or literary, aspect of the principle of scripture as its own interpreter. This means that more difficult parts should be explained from the simpler. This was already an accepted principle of interpretation in the schools of rhetoric, and one which we all use; when we come to a difficult passage in a book we read on to get the overall sense of the writer in order to interpret the difficult passage more accurately. Thus Luther, writing against Erasmus, can say

> Truly it is stupid and impious, when we know that the subject matter of Scripture has all been placed in the clearest light, to call it obscure on account of a few obscure words. If the words are obscure in the one place, yet they are plain in another.[20]

In his actual exegesis Luther uses this principle; when Erasmus produced arguments in favour of free will Luther pointed out that his interpretation did not fit in with the rest of scripture;[21] equally he used the same principle against Zwingli's arguments in relation to the presence of Christ in the eucharist.[22]

As time went by in each case it was on the second meaning of each of the two principles that scholars fastened. They sought the literal sense and understood it as the sense which the writer intended; they interpreted difficult texts by those which were clearer. It was the adoption of these understandings of the two principles which led directly, though over a long passage of time, to the historical-critical method.[23]

---

[19] *Bondage*, 261 = *WA* 18.733.
[20] *Op. cit.* 110f. = *WA* 18.606.
[21] *Op. cit.* 183 = *WA* 18.672.
[22] Cf. J. Pelikan, *Luther's Works: Luther the Expositor*, 127f.
[23] A Polish Socinian Catechism of 1680 enunciates four principles of interpretation. (1) The purpose and other circumstances of the text must be considered in the case of scripture as with all other authors (this implies that scripture is interpreted in the same way as other books). (2) A careful comparison with similar and clearer expressions and concepts should be set out. (3) The interpretation of difficult passages is to be checked with those places where the meaning of the writing is clear; nothing is to be allowed which diverges from these. (4) Nothing is to be asserted which contradicts *sana ratio* or which contains a contradiction in itself (see K. Scholder, *Ursprünge und Probleme der Bibelkritik im 17. Jahrhundert*, München 1966, 47).

Before we go on to examine the ultimate result of accepting these principles consider for a moment some of the difficulties which lie in each of the principles understood according to their second meanings.

What precisely do we mean by the literal sense? Most of the scholars of the middle ages and the Reformation understood by it the re-discovery of the sense intended by the author.[24] But if the author is writing in a language other than his first language he may not be able to express himself in the way he would wish to; if Mark was an Aramaic-speaking Palestinian this may explain some of the difficulties in his gospel. Embarrassment with the subject with which he is dealing often makes a writer unclear; many have believed that Paul when he came to write about the circumcision of Titus in Gal. 2: 3 was under such emotional stress that he wrote clumsily and so left us in considerable doubt as to what he really meant. It may also be that words themselves, even in the hands of the greatest of masters, may not be adequate for the task to which they are set; thus praise of God may fall far short of what the writer intends simply because words fail him. If God's appearance cannot be carved in stone or wood can his activity be adequately depicted in words?

An author may also deliberately use words in order to conceal his intention. In ecclesiastical meetings it is customary for those who dislike innovations suggested by the young to propose that in view of the importance of the proposed reform it ought to be referred to a committee, knowing well that once in a committee it will either be forgotten or so wrapped up in a committee report as to be ineffective. There may also be levels of meaning in the words a writer uses. There will be a basic meaning but the words will also carry overtones and undertones of which the writer himself may not have been conscious.

[24]Cf. *Bondage*, 193f = *WA* 18.679 f.

Schleiermacher's dictum is appropriate here 'To understand the text at first as well as and then even better than its author'.[25] The psychologists have shown us that there are such levels of meaning and that they influence us in the subconscious or unconscious areas of our minds.

Finally the adoption of the literal sense brings back the difficulties which the allegorical sense was designed to remove. Luther observed differences between the gospels but was not greatly disturbed by them; their main purpose is to testify to Christ and not to provide reliable history.[26] Faced with contradictions and impossibilities in scripture Calvin adopted one or other of two ways of interpretation. In respect of the divergence between the synoptic gospels and the fourth gospel about the date of the crucifixion, Calvin argued that Jesus kept the Passover on the correct day as given in the synoptics but that the Jews had a custom that when the Passover preceded the Sabbath it should be moved one day forward so that there would not be two successive days without work. This Jewish custom cannot be substantiated but Calvin believed it could and accepted it as an explanation.[27]

Calvin solved other difficulties, and the anthropomorphisms and immoralities, by the principle of accommodation.[28] God is our teacher and like any good teacher he accommodates himself to his hearers. If scripture speaks of God as having a mouth or ears it is because God speaks 'baby talk' to us as nurses commonly do with infants; such forms of speaking do not in so much express clearly the nature of God as accommodate our knowledge of him to the weakness of our minds.[29]

[25] *Hermeneutics: The Handwritten Manuscripts*, (ed. H. Kimmerle; ET by J. Duke and J. Forstmann), 112.
[26] Cf. *WA* 17.184, 179.
[27] See Matt. 26:14-20 in his *Harmony of the Gospels (CR 73)*.
[28] Cf. F. L. Battles, 'God was Accommodating Himself to Human Capacity', *Interpretation* 31, 1977, 19-38. Theodore of Mopsuestia had already accepted and used this principle.
[29] *Institutes* I. 13.1.

Sometimes however Calvin simply accepts contradictions. Matthew and Luke place the cleansing of the temple on the day Jesus entered Jerusalem; Mark puts it on the next day. Calvin reconciles these by saying that when Mark 'saw he had not spoken of a cleansing of the temple he put it in later, out of place . . . afterwards he recalls the omission which deserved to be told'.[30]

The second principle, scripture as its own interpreter, also requires careful definition. Because scripture is written in a foreign language we need to use a dictionary to understand and though the dictionary may actually restrict itself to words in the New Testament and call itself a New Testament dictionary it in fact depends upon larger dictionaries which cover the whole of Greek literature. Our understanding of the words and the grammatical constructions used in the New Testament depend on our wider knowledge of the Greek language. If we did not make use of this knowledge then we would be like cipher experts faced in war with a new code used by the enemy; any understanding must come from breaking into it and reading it from inside. Now it may be that in one sense of the principle, the sense which sees scripture as a closed circle written by the Holy Spirit, it is necessary to have the Christian experience in order to understand, yet this is not so in respect of the sense of the principle with which we are now concerned. Indeed the reformers themselves made ample use of their knowledge of the languages in which scripture was written in order to advance their understanding of it. While so much is

---

[30]See his *Harmony of the Gospels* (ET by A. W. Morrison), Edinburgh 1972 = *CR* 73, *ad loc.* The first of the reformers who refused to allow any divergences among the gospels was Osiander who compiled a Harmony and attempted to fit everything in. He thus had Jesus heal four blind men at Jericho (to Calvin's scorn). See G. Müller, 'Osianders "Evangelienharmonie"', in *Histoire de l'exégèse au XVIe siècle* (ed. O. Fatio and P. Fraenkel), Genève 1978, 256-64. For the absurdities of the patristic period see H. Merkel, *Widersprüche zwischen den Evangelien*, Tübingen 1971.

clear in respect of the grammar and anyone would concede it, what about the concepts and ideas which appear in scripture? Can they be understood wholly within the ambit of the bible or do we need to go outside it in order to understand? It is the clear answer of scholarship that we must go outside.

Finally in respect of the principles we have discussed it is implicit that when they have been properly used what appears through them out of scripture is God's Word, what God intended men to hear. Thus Luther writes "Our first concern will be for the grammatical meaning for this is the truly theological meaning'.[31] The difficulties inherent in such a view will appear later. It should be clear from what I have said that to be able to use these two principles it is necessary to know as much as possible about the ancient world. Both Luther and Calvin make use of the knowledge, admittedly very slight, and often very erroneous, which existed of it. But very soon the deliberate search for more information began. Grotius (1583-1645) was amongst the first of many to collect parallels from Greek and Roman literature to the words and ideas of the New Testament. John Lightfoot (1602-1675) searched Jewish rabbinic writings for parallels to the gospels and Paul.[32] The work however was spasmodic until the nineteenth century. The rise of historical science with its desire to discover what really happened led in everything associated with history to an increased emphasis on original material. The archaeologist

---

[31] WA 5.27 (quoted in G. Ebeling, *Luther*, London 1970, 107).

[32] J. J. Wettstein (1693-1754) expresses this very well:

If you wish to get a thorough and complete understanding of the books of the New Testament, put yourself in the place of those to whom they were first delivered by the Apostles as a legacy. Transfer yourself in thought to that time and area where they first were read. Endeavour, so far as possible, to acquaint yourself with the customs, practices, habits, opinions, accepted ways of thought, proverbs, symbolic language and everyday expressions of these men, and with the ways and means by which they attempt to persuade others or to furnish a firm foundation for faith. Above all, keep in mind, when you turn to a passage, that you can make no progress by means of any modern system, whether of theology or of logic, or by means of opinions current today (quoted in W. G. Kümmel, *The New Testament*, 50).

searched for the remains of past civilisations; the scholar examined contemporary documents for what light they might throw on the culture and civilisation of their age. Great advances were made and so by the end of the nineteenth century it was possible for painters to represent fairly accurately the dress of people living in the first century. Much more importantly their customs, thought patterns and ways of behaviour became clear.

The painting can be more accurate; the original intention of those who pushed for the literal or plain sense of the words is being fulfilled. But has the New Testament been brought any nearer? Was the sixteenth century better off because it did not see the difference between the dress of a Roman soldier and the dress of a contemporary soldier? If Jesus was set in a contemporary scene wearing contemporary dress was he not nearer to those who saw the picture? If we answer 'Yes' we have at the same time to confess that what was a possibility in the sixteenth century is not a possibility today. Even at the very lowest levels of education people are aware that there is a difference between our world and the world of the first century. If we present Jesus in twentieth century dress they will complain. Anyone who produces a nativity play is faced with this dilemma: are the characters to be dressed in modern clothes and made to speak with modern idiom or are they to be presented as people who lived in a different time from ourselves in the clothes of that time? If we depict Jesus in clothes contemporary with us we deny the historicity of the incarnation; if we depict him in first century dress we deny its contemporanity. Jesus both belongs to history and is a man of our time.

It was assumed by those who pursued the literal meaning of scripture leading on to the historical-critical method that given a more accurate picture of the ancient world it would be possible to determine more correctly what the text meant so that various controversies could be settled. The method was not pursued by protestants solely because they wished to confound catholics but often because they needed to settle some of their own internal differences. A better understanding of the text would enable them to decide whether baptism of believers or infant baptism was the method scripture intended. However more accurate understanding of the text has not led to a solution of this problem. The fault in part lies in the inadequacy of information provided by scripture, but it lies even more with the interpreter. When an interpreter comes to scripture he can neither get himself out of the way nor can he clear away the past centuries of interpretation so that he can approach the text with a fresh and clear mind. In other words a neutral academic approach is impossible. The scientist assumes when he has proposed a theory that anyone who follows through his work will be persuaded by the evidence to reach exactly the same conclusion. The historian may hope that this will happen but he knows that he can never assume it. The biblical historian, because of the way in which he and his fellows are emotionally tied to their subject, can be even less sure that those who follow the steps of his argument will come to the same conclusion. Thus the pursuit of the literal sense into the historical-critical sense has not led to a resolution of all the questions put to scripture by its readers.

However it must be acknowledged that many of the original difficulties no longer perturb those who work today at scripture. They no longer worry where Cain got his wife or are scandalised by Samuel hacking Agag in pieces; divergences between the gospels on factual, and even on theological matters, do not disturb them. The historical-critical method has thus not only brought a much more detailed and vivid picture of the ancient world and a more reliable understanding of what the biblical characters said and did, but it has also removed many of the problems which led to allegorisation in earlier days. All this represents an undoubted success.

Before going further it is necessary to look at what happened to the second of the two Reformation hermeneutical principles: scripture as its own interpreter. The search for parallels which would enlighten the meaning of scripture was, as we have seen, extended beyond scripture itself. This led to the recognition that scripture would have to be treated in the same way as any other book. This, urged with increasing emphasis by scholars, became generally accepted in the nineteenth century as an essential foundation for historical work. If then scripture is to be interpreted against a wider historical context than its own content, how wide is that context to be? To understand the Greek historian Thucydides we make use of all we can learn from any source about fifth century Athens and we do not start from an assumption that any particular piece of evidence or literature is inherently more valuable than another; we only reach this conclusion about some strand of material after we have examined and tested its reliability. If all contemporary evidence must be used for the interpretation of a particular author is this to hold true for the bible? Strict adherence to the principle that scripture is its own interpreter would mean that when we searched for the Jewish background to a New Testament passage we should look only at the Old Testament. But Jewish thought contemporary with the New Testament continued to develop after the writing of the last section of the Old Testament. Jude vv. 14-15 quotes 1 Enoch 1.9 indicating that the New Testament itself does not restrict itself to the canonical Old Testament. Qumran literature throws much light on the New Testament. It and the apocalyptic literature are outside Jewish canonical literature, yet we use them equally with the canon in understanding the New Testament. Should we not go outside Jewish literature altogether? The discovery of Gnostic material at Nag Hammadi is comparable to that made at Qumran. But even before that discovery a great deal of other ancient literature was used in understanding the New Testament. Is scripture then to be understood as a part of world culture and explained in its terms and not just in its own terms? The religious historical school clearly moved into the position where scripture was assumed to be a part of human existence and to be understood as a part of the developing consciousness of man.

At the same time it became clear that there were contradictions of varying degrees of importance within scripture. The internal harmony of scripture could no longer be maintained and the Holy Spirit no longer seen in any simple sense as its author. If that understanding of the unity of scripture disappears so also does the dogmatic understanding of the principle of scripture as its own interpreter.[33]

In a real sense the original position has been reversed: scripture as divinely inspired to be interpreted from within itself has become scripture as part of the culture and literature of the world to be understood within and out of that culture and literature. Thus the historical-critical method has led to the retention of one principle of the reformers, the literal sense in its non-dogmatic aspect, and to the dropping of the other, scripture as its own interpreter, indeed to its reversal. The scholar has now become the interpreter of scripture. Truth is no longer revealed to the foolish and the children.

Certainly the work of scholars who treated the New Testament as they would have treated any other book has brought many advantages and greatly aided the understanding of the New Testament.[34] Not least it has broken the shackles of dogmatism and set the historical Jesus free. Once again he has

---

[33]The dogmatic understanding of the principle disappeared as soon as the Old and New Testaments began to be treated independently. Theodore of Mopsuestia approached this position but it was not until Turretini (1671-1737) that it was explicitly argued in respect of the New Testament; cf. O. Merk, 'Anfänge neutestamentliche Wissenschaft im 18. Jahrhundert' in *Historische Kritik in der Theologie* (ed. G. Schwaiger), Göttingen 1980, 37-59.

[34]Again Turretini appears to have been the first to make this point explicitly; so Kümmel, *op. cit.* 58.

become a living figure and not merely the subject of dogmatic statements. The scholar has no longer to move within tramlines set down by the dogmatists and ensure that his interpretation always lies within these lines. There have also been dramatic losses. My original illustration may have suggested that the differences between our century and the first were only external, changes in dress, in weapons of warfare, in modes of transport. The differences go far deeper. The world of the sixteenth and seventeenth centuries was much more like the world of the first century than the world of the twentieth century is like that of either the sixteenth or the first. It was thus easy for those in the sixteenth century to think of their world as so similar to that of the first century that they could apply directly to their own situation the precepts of scripture and understand theological doctrine in the terms of the early church. In large part the philosophies by which they lived derived their meaning from the philosophies which held sway during the first few centuries of the Christian era. In other words the literal meaning could reveal the Word of God to the sixteenth century in almost the same terms as it did to the first century, though minor adaptations might need to be made. Luther transferred Paul's attacks on legalism into attacks on the catholic church, but in terms of the prevailing abuses this was not too difficult to do.

What significant changes then have taken place between our century and the first? It is only possible to indicate these briefly. Jerusalem is no longer regarded as the centre of the universe; with a somewhat natural arrogance astronomers moved the base line for longtitude from Jerusalem to Greenwich; the earth itself is now seen as a very minor planet in a vast universe; our perspective on ourselves and our relation to the universe has therefore changed greatly. Under the influence of Descartes philosophy took as its starting point man rather than God and from what seemed to be the sure existence of the philosopher himself it considered the universe and its meaning. The biological sciences soon showed to man that not even was he not unique but that he was continuous with nature and therefore not a special creation of God. These changes were known before this century. The most important changes in this century have probably to be associated with the technology that has opened a vast range of new possibilities; these possibilities have opened up new moral questions. Contraception and abortion which previously carried great risks now became safe and a matter of course for rich and poor alike. It is assumed that if technology shows that anything can be done it is right to do it; if nuclear generators can be built then it is right to build them.

All this means that people today look at the world in a quite different way from people in the first century. When a car will not start its owner opens the bonnet, pokes around for a little while, and if he cannot find out what is wrong, sends for a mechanic. Had he lived in the first century he would probably have assumed that a spell had been put on it and sent for a magician. If a businessman in the ancient world wanted to know whether he should launch a new product on the market he would have taken the omens, examined the entrails of a bird or consulted an astrologist; today he would call in an advertising firm to prepare a campaign, employ something like the Gallup organisation to carry out a market survey in one small area of the country and then in the light of the results make his decision. The supernatural has been banished from the ordinary areas of life.

At the same time completely new questions have come over the horizon for which answers are needed. Scripture was written in a society where goods were scarce; we live in an abundant society. Scripture assumed that everyone would work; we are rapidly moving away from any such idea. It looks as if there are already young people who have left school at 16 and will never have worked when they start to draw their pension at 65. Even those who work will discover that their hours of work will grow less; the micro-chip is easing people out of the need to work eight hours every day. How will they spend their leisure?

Modernising a biblical play by putting the characters in modern dress or making them speak with modern idioms does not answer questions of this sort. New scenes, almost new plays, are required. The leaders of the protestant Reformation assumed the similarity of the first and sixteenth centuries and stressing the literal sense of scripture thereby hoped to obtain guidance for the problems with which they were faced. The historical-critical method deriving ultimately from their biblical principles has displayed a great gap between the ancient world and our world. Where do we go from here?

We must be careful however not to over-emphasise the gap between the world of the first century and our world. There is a continuity both of culture between the two worlds and of interpretation of scripture in the life of the church. These continuities help to bridge the gulf. We should also note that there is much which is still as relevant to our era as it was to the first century, e.g. sayings of Jesus applying to the personal sphere. 'Whoever would save his life shall lose it and whoever will lose his life for my sake and the gospel's will save it' still remains true even though the world in which life is to be lost is very different.

The historical-critical method presupposes the neutrality of its exponents. No interpreter is in fact neutral. As part of this we must recognise that we belong to the twentieth century and our understanding of an ancient text belongs to the twentieth century. An illustration may help. There are those who wish to hear eighteenth century music as eighteenth century music was heard in the eighteenth century. They therefore use instruments made in that century and arrangements which were current then. But they can never hear with eighteenth century ears. They have already heard the music with twentieth century instruments and this colours the way in which they listen to the eighteenth century instruments. The hearer of the eighteenth century had only heard eighteenth century instruments and had never heard the difference which twentieth century instruments make. Even if a twentieth century musician were to hear a fresh early piece of music on eighteenth century instruments he would still not be hearing as someone in the eighteenth century would hear for he has been brought up to listen to twentieth century instruments for almost all the music he hears. He can never genuinely return to the eighteenth century. Perhaps the interpreter of scripture has an advantage here; the only interpretation which is meaningful is one which can be understood in the twentieth century. To interpret he must interpret into the twentieth century.

But again we must note that the literal meaning once it has been found by the historical-critical method may simply be inapplicable to us. There is no way in which we can move from the advice given in scripture to slaves to an adequate consideration of the relationship of trade unions to employers.

The historical-critical method is here and here to stay; we use it but we are not satisfied with it. Again and again students express their dissatisfaction with the teaching of the New Testament. It is the great temptation of its teachers to stop with the literal meaning as deduced by historical-criticism and go no further. That leaves the impression that the literal meaning is the meaning today. Teaching however which stops there is not only inadequate but also misleading. How can we go further?

The basic error in protestantism's use of the method seems to have been the idea that scripture could be a guide book to life. Luther said that scripture contained the Word of God as a cradle contains a baby; it is the baby and not the cradle which is important. In practice he often transgressed this and by the third generation of reformers the simple equation was being made: the Word of God equals the words of scripture. It is quite easy to see that such a view accords with the stressing of the literal meaning. That the protestants took it in this way can be seen very easily from the way in which they used scripture as a model for church organisation and claimed that the particular ecclesiastical structure to which they adhered was in accordance with scripture. Such a view was pardonable in writers of the sixteenth century, especially in view of the likeness of their world and its problems to that of the first century. Pardonable in them, it is unpardonable in us; and it is the historical-critical method that brings us to see this. Its principal importance is not that it shows us that certain books in the New Testament were written by others than their traditional authors or that they date from different periods than they themselves seem to suggest, but that the world of the New Testament is very different from our world. Scripture then becomes inadequate for the task for which those who stressed 'the literal meaning' and 'scripture as its own interpreter' hoped it would be the answer.

A new approach to the nature of scripture is needed.[35] Some have been attracted by finding a core principle within scripture from which the whole is understood, a canon within a canon; Luther took his bearings for the rest of scripture from the principle of justification by faith and accorded, as it were, prizes to different parts of scripture in so far as they contained this principle. Harnack thought of a core of truths, the fatherhood of God, the brotherhood of man, the immortality of the soul. It was a view which suited the age in which he lived but is so time-conditioned in its expression that it seems

---

[35]A view of the canon is implicit here; I have treated this in 'Scripture, Tradition and the Canon of the New Testament' (The Manson Memorial Lecture, Manchester 1979), within pp. 14ff.

hopelessly outdated to us. Dodd unearthed a central kerygma; but there seems to be more than one kerygma in the New Testament; in any case Dodd did not himself accept as true all the kerygma which he had discovered. If we reject such methods what then do we say?

It is only possible to give a few hints of the way we may go. The writings of the New Testament were the responses of men participating in the Christian experience to the situations in which they found themselves; they sought to bring Christ into their situations. In a very similar way interpretation of scripture must be the bringing of scripture by men of Christian experience into the situations of today. That is mis-stated. In the end it is not scripture which the Christian interprets but what God has done in Israel and in Christ. Put in more traditional protestant terms the task of the exegete is to bring the Word of God into our lives. Scripture contains the Word of God as it was directed to the Corinthians or the Romans; it is not sufficient to understand what the Word said to them; we must know what it is saying to us.

This means that there is no direct way of using scripture. We cannot pick it up and without more ado apply it to our world. We cannot and ought not to try to extrapolate from it to where we are. We have situations which we cannot reach from scripture by moving backwards, forwards or sideways. What we have to do is to go back through scripture to that to which scripture is a response. I shall not define that to which scripture is the response other than to say that it is the activity of God in Israel and Jesus. Any attempt to define it is itself time-conditioned, and that means conditioned by the time in which it is made and not in the time of the ancient world. Such a view also implies that scripture cannot be set aside; it is indispensible. But having gone back through scripture we need to come forward to where we are and we can do this because the God to whom we have gone back is the God who lives today. How we in fact come forward is quite another matter and would take a lecture or a course of lectures.[36] In a real sense it is not something which New Testament scholars, or Old Testament scholars, are able to do. Much more than detailed exegesis is necessary. Clearly the latter is necessary for if we have to go back through scripture then we must know everything we can about scripture. This we learn from the historical-critical method.

Very briefly three things may be said:

(1) It is only possible to come forward within a consciously held total theological and philosophical position. When we look at the great interpreters of the past we find that they were not just great academic scholars but that they worked from a systematic position in theology and philosophy.[37]

(2) It can only be carried out in the church. A Jew, even an agnostic, can use the historical-critical method and unearth what Paul was saying in the first century to the Galatians.[38] It is only someone standing within the church and upheld by the church who can speak to the church what God says to it today.

(3) It can only be done by one who has a genuine sensitivity towards, and deep knowledge of, the world. This may exclude all those who work in academic circles. We cannot bring God to the world unless we know the world to which he must be brought.

[36]I have tried to treat this in *From Test to Sermon* (2nd edn. T. & T. Clark, Edinburgh, 1988).

[37]Long ago Tertullian argued that all interpretation should take place within the rule of faith, cf. *De Praescriptione Haereticorum*, 13, 14. This puts a limit on speculation as also do protestant fundamentalists when they say that 'These are the principles of the faith' and imply that all interpretation must take place within them. But if we lay down rigorous principles within which scripture must be interpreted in time the principles become absolute; they are no longer examined from scripture itself and so are no longer open to change as Christ is encountered in new ages.

[38]Yet anyone can draw existential meaning from any text of the past; Christians and non-Christians can be led to reflect on present human situations through reading Shakespeare; the non-Christian can be forced to re-think his own position without becoming a Christian through the reading of scripture.

4

ON DEFINING THE CENTRAL MESSAGE OF THE NEW TESTAMENT

Few teachers of the New Testament have escaped the question as to the heart, core or centre of their subject. At some time or other some student will ask the question. As a result the divinity classrooms of the world are knee deep in discarded definitions. I do not propose to add to that depth. I only wish to raise some of the preliminary issues which must be considered before any attempt is made to seek a central message or heart to the New Testament. In this way I shall avoid laying my head on the block and I hope also fulfil the terms of this lectureship in avoiding subjects of theological controversy. Before I go further I would express my gratitude to the University of London for its invitation to deliver this lecture and for the honour it has done me in allowing my name to be added to the long line of distinguished lecturers.

I shall look first at the need to discuss our question, then at some of the attempts which have been thought to answer it and finally at some of the issues which these attempts raise.

I

Two centuries ago no one would have thought our question worthy of discussion but the rise of the historical critical method and its application to the study of the New Testament has changed all that. We are now aware of the diversity of the material in the New Testament.[1] This has created an acute

---

[1]For detailed discussion of diversity see e.g. John Charlot, *New Testament Disunity*, E. P. Dutton & Co., New York, 1970; J. D. G. Dunn, *Unity and Diversity in the New Testament*, S.C.M., London, 1977.

problem both for those who attribute normative value to its writings and also for those who because of curriculum requirements have to teach the book as an existing unity. In turning now to outline briefly the diversity within the New Testament I am not concerned with the diversity of literary material, letters, gospels, accounts of miracles, sermons and all the rest. The diversity which causes trouble is that of factual statement and theological view.

There are factual differences which are difficult to reconcile. Did Jesus cleanse the temple on the day he entered Jerusalem as in Matthew or on the day after as in Mark? Did he die at the time of the slaughter of the passover lambs as in John or had he eaten the passover as in the Synoptic Gospels? Can Paul's account of the struggle over the admission of Gentiles be reconciled with that of Acts? These divergences may seem of little importance to scholars and of value only in providing material for examination questions but as anyone who has had to deal with lay people who have discovered them will know they can cause great heart burnings. There is no need now to deal with either their reconciliation or their actual unimportance.

Of greater significance are the divergences in theological outlook within the various writings of the New Testament. Since Luther's day it has been traditional to put forward a possible divergence between Paul and James as the most likely candidate for discussion. There are now many other candidates. In using Mark Luke eliminates his statements giving soteriological significance to the death of Jesus. Jesus dies as martyr, witness and hero rather than to save men from their sins. There is then, not unexpectedly, a considerable difference between the picture which Luke presents in Acts of Paul and his theology from that which we gain from his own letters. Apart from differences of chronology between John and the Synoptics they diverge considerably in the picture they offer of

Jesus in that in John he talks so much more about himself and his position as Son of God. There are again differences between the soteriologies of John and Paul.[2] If we read Romans chapter 13 and Revelation chapter 13 we encounter differing responses to the way in which Christians should view the state. Finally there are differing views about the nearness of the parousia, and that even within one writer, Paul.

I make no attempt to detail or defend any of these differences. They are amply discussed in the standard textbooks; even those who would play them down, if not deny their existence, indicate by the amount of attention they give them that they constitute a serious problem. If the New Testament had been a systematic theology written by one person, or even by a group of people who met together to discuss what should go into it, there might have been no problem. The diversity is caused in the first place by the situationally conditioned nature of each of the New Testament books. There cannot then be any easy harmonisation and we must expect to find, at the very least, the same truth expressed in different ways. Because of the differences in Jewish and Hellenistic culture a Jew and a Greek would affirm the importance of Jesus to themselves with different words and thought forms, though there might indeed be little over which they would quarrel if each thoroughly understood the thought of the other.

However there are deeper reasons for diversity than the situational nature of the writings of the New Testament. There may be different understandings of what Plato wrote; there are much greater differences in respect of Socrates because we do not have direct access to him but can only approach him through the writings of others. We do not have direct access to

[2]E.g. see R. Schnackenburg, 'Paulinische und Johanneische Christologie: Ein Vergleich' in *Die Mitte des Neuen Testaments* (Festschrift für Eduard Schweizer, ed. U. Luz and H. Weder), Vandenhoeck & Ruprecht, Gottingen, 1983, pp. 221-237.

Jesus. But, and this is significant, those who did have direct
access to his disciples were compelled to change their view of
him after his resurrection. Then they saw his life as a whole and
saw that it harmonised with his teaching.[3] Believing in his
resurrection they viewed him from a wholly new perspective.[4]
What they have handed on to us is not then a series of responses
to his teaching in fresh situations, as Islamic scholars may be
said to have done with the teaching of Mohammed. In order
to come to terms with what they believed had happened they
had to take up categories and concepts that are not normal to
logical and scientific thought. Even Jesus' death in full accord
with his teaching now took on a changed significance as they
saw in it their own salvation from sin and victory over the
supernatural powers which previously had governed their
destinies. Uncharted ways lay before them and it was natural
that they should move along different paths as they sought to
accommodate what had happened in Jesus with the old and
new problems they encountered day by day.

   If then diversity was inevitable it also has its value for those
who believe that their faith and behaviour should be guided by
the New Testament, not to speak of its value for those who year
by year have to set examination questions. Our situations,
culture and world view are in many respects very different from
those of the first century. Were we faced with a monolithic set
of writings all coming from the same situation and culture and
possessing the same world view then we would find it difficult
to know how to make the transition from that position to our
own and so how to use the New Testament as a primary source
for our lives. The variety of response to changing circumstances within the New Testament gives us a first clue as to the

³Cf. P. Pokorný, *Die Entstehung der Christologie*, Calwer Verlag, Stuttgart, 1985. (E.T.
The Genesis of Christology, T&T Clark, Edinburgh 1987.)
   ⁴Cf. U. Luz, 'Einheit und Vielfalt neutestamentlicher Theologien' in *Die Mitte des Neuen
Testaments* (see n. 2), pp. 142-161.

ways in which we ourselves may respond to that to which the New Testament writers were responding when they wrote their books. When we see the theological presuppositions that led Mark, Paul, John and Peter to adopt particular answers to their problems we are more easily able to see the answers which we should be offering to our own. The view of the state presented in Revelation 13 has enabled the church to endure in many situations of persecution; the view presented in Romans 13 was useful to me in a border parish in Northern Ireland where smuggling was rife: the law must be obeyed! This aside the variety within the New Testament also saves us from a narrow dogmatism in theological assertion. If the primitive church could accept differing opinions may not we? This is of great importance in the ecumenical area where contending churches sometimes adopt the position: unless, our view is accepted we will not play ball.

Once we grasp the extent of the diversity in the New Testament we may feel like asking whether there is a central message at all. This question was asked in an extreme form last century when it was argued that Paul was a second founder of Christianity and indeed its real founder in the form in which we know it. He had perverted the simple religion of Jesus into a mystery cult. Few, if any, would hold this view today. I shall therefore assume in what follows that there is a central message and offer only two sustaining arguments: (i) Those who brought together the writings of the New Testament in the second to fifth centuries believed they contained a common message which made them into a unity. (ii) In some way all the writings reflect the teaching, personality, life, death and resurrection of Jesus. I am not arguing that the early church made the best selection of what was available; perhaps some of what it included ought to have been eliminated and other material included. We cannot deal with this issue for most of the material no longer exists. Paul's own letters show we do not possess all he wrote (1 Cor. 5.9; 2 Cor. 2.3; 7.8). If we had access to the writings on which Luke in his prologue says he depended (1.1-4) we might prefer them. None of this however can be taken to imply that there is not some kind of unity within the present canonical New Testament.

Before we go on to examine some of the statements of the central message I would like to reinforce any doubts you may have as to the difficulty of the task. Within Protestantism it has been traditional to see Paul, if not as the centre of the New Testament, at least as very close to it. This was perhaps satisfactory in the days when there was agreement as to Paul's central message, that of the justification of the sinner by God's grace through Christ. But today not even Protestant scholars are agreed that this is the centre of his thought. Schweitzer found it in his Christ-mysticism.[5] R. P. Martin finds it in the theme of reconciliation.[6] There is no need to explore these views. I only mention them to underline the difficulties of our task. Equal difficulties would appear if we set out to state the central theme of the teaching of Jesus or of the theology of John. If we cannot agree on the central theme of any one writer in the New Testament is it likely that we shall agree on that of the whole New Testament?

II

I now go on to examine some statements of the central message.[7] My approach will be neither systematic nor chrono-

---

[5] A. Schweitzer, *The Mysticism of Paul the Apostle* (E.T. W. Montgomery), London, A. & C. Black, 1931.

[6] R. P. Martin, *Reconciliation: A Study of Paul's Theology*, Marshall, Morgan and Scott, London, 1981.

[7] Alan Richardson wrote in the Preface to his *An Introduction to the Theology of the New Testament* (S.C.M., London 1958), p. 10 'We must all have *some* (italics his) notion at the back of our minds about the meaning of the New Testament as a whole, and it is just as well that some people should try to say what it is'. I for my part am happy to examine what others have written without necessarily agreeing with their proposals.

logical. The statements I have selected are chosen not for their intrinsic or historical value but because they open up the presuppositions underlying any attempt to deal with it. I do not intend to criticise all or any of them in detail but only in so far as this will assist us in our search for the underlying questions which require our attention. Few of those I shall mention in fact set out to answer our question but they gave implicit answers which rightly or wrongly have been regarded by others as statements of the central message of the New Testament.

(1) Clearly one way of producing an easily stated unity within the New Testament is to cut down on its variety. Historically the first person consciously to adopt this method was Marcion through his elimination of anything that did not fit with his picture of Paul. However Luther's attempt to do the same has been of much greater significance, and there are many who still follow it.

Luther regarded as of primary importance John's Gospel, I John, the letters of Paul, especially those to the Romans, Galatians and Ephesians, and I Peter. In his translation of the New Testament he placed James, Hebrews, Jude and Revelation in a kind of appendix. The remaining books fell into some in-between category. The criterion he employed was whether a book did or did not preach Christ. However to say that a book preaches Christ is very difficult to express in a way with which everyone will agree. What one scholar or churchman regards as preaching Christ will be disputed by another, as can be observed when any serious dispute arises about the faith of the church. Luther was thus compelled to go on and associate with the preaching of Christ the doctrine of justification by grace. This in fact then became for him the central message.

It does not take us long to discover difficulties with this solution. (i) Quite apart from it being regarded as the main thrust of the New Testament there is as we have seen no

agreement that it is the main thrust of Paul. (ii) It is doubtful
if John would have known what we were talking about if we
had told him this was what his Gospel was really about. (iii)
Paul formulated his teaching on justification over against
certain views he found among Jewish Christians on the continuing validity of the Jewish Law for all Christians. Granted
he was correct in rejecting these views not all heretics are
Judaizers. There may be difficulties in refuting other heresies
if we have always to begin from a doctrine of justification by
faith. Luther probably only selected justification by faith as
central because the views he found in the Catholic church of
his day appeared to be very similar to those he found rejected
in Paul's letters. (iv) The doctrine of justification by faith is
essentially individualistic in outlook for it speaks of individuals
being right in the sight of God. Many of our problems today
arise out of our social culture and are basically social rather than
individualistic. An individualistic central doctrine may not
then be a good starting point from which to tackle them. (v)
In Luther's day the question 'How can I be right with God?'
was important. The penances and indulgences against which
he protested had been designed to deal with this issue. How
many people in Western civilisation today are worried at all
about their stance before God? These criticisms begin to open
up for us the wider issues which are involved in any statement
of the central message of the New Testament. For that reason
I have given them greater attention than I shall give to the views
of others.

(2) I need only allude briefly to what in one sense appears to
be the opposite solution to that of Luther. For many liberal
theologians of last century Paul was cast aside and the central
message of the New Testament became the teaching of Jesus.
Their faith lay in the historical Jesus rather than the Pauline
Christ. This historical Jesus was one wholly denuded of
traditional theological dogma and devoid of any trace of

supernatural colouring. Since the Jesus these scholars found by use of historical methods is no longer one acceptable today it is unnecessary to do other than to point out that they discovered their 'central message' by concentrating on the synoptic Gospels from which they derived eternal principles and by ignoring all other parts of the New Testament. Like Luther they first selected an internal canon but came up with a very different result because the selected canon was different.

(3) A third way of dealing with the problem is simply to ignore it and to assume that every writer in the New Testament held the same basic view. Since it is normally extreme right-wing conservatives who adopt this solution they tend to discover traditional Protestantism reflected in every part of the New Testament. If Luke omitted certain soteriological sayings of Jesus which he found in Mark he did so because his readers already knew Mark and he did not need to repeat what was in that Gospel. Similarly when Luke wrote about Paul he assumed his readers knew Paul's letters and therefore did not need to give in detail his theological position. This is a caricature and it would be difficult to find any thinking conservative who would hold it. To ignore the problem will not make it go away. Traditional Catholics of course have never needed to produce a solution since they are not interested so much in the central message of the New Testament as they are in that of the church.

(4) Our next possible solution was much in vogue in the days when Biblical Theology reigned supreme. One of the brief statements of primitive belief which are contained within the New Testament is selected and taken to represent the church's kerygma. It is assumed that it ought to be possible to discover within Scripture a statement in its own terms expressing its essential message.[8] Before instancing possible passages it is

---

[8]Related to this approach are those who see the message of the New Testament encapsulated in one particular verse. For a brief selection of suggested verses see N. M. Watson,

important to look at the underlying assumption of this approach, and indeed of much writing on our subject. As Kümmel says, though not in picking out a primitive creed but in defence of his choice of Jesus, Paul and John as the key witnesses, 'We can expect to encounter this witness in its purest version in those forms of primitive Christian proclamation which stand closest in point of time to the historical Christ event'.[9] Is it true that the earliest will be the purest? A moment's reflection will show that this is certainly not true of experience in general. My immediate reaction to some of the statements of politicians with whom I disagree is to grow hot under the collar but after I have cooled down I may be prepared to allow that there is something in what they say; after some years I may even allow that they were actually right! Turning more directly to our own area when we look at the primitive church we quickly discover changing views. It was only after a bitter fight that the earliest view that Gentiles could not become Christians unless they first adopted Jewish ways was held to be false. The earliest was not here the purest! Even if we moved to a slightly later period, say around AD 55, and conducted a poll of Christian thought, the majority view might still have been that of Jewish Christianity.[10] That no primitive creed incorporating such a view has survived may simply represent the victory of the other side.

We look then at some of the kerygmatic statements that have been offered and at some that might have been offered, if the searchers' own theology had not predetermined their

---

'... To make us rely not on ourselves but on God who raises the dead' in *Die Mitte des Neuen Testaments* (see n. 2), pp. 384-398 at p. 388. He himself suggests 2 Cor. 1.9b. To his list we may add W. G. Kümmel, *The Theology of the New Testament* (E.T. J. E. Steely, Abingdon, Nashville and New York, 1973), p. 333 who selects Heb. 13.8.

[9]Op. cit., p. 324.

[10]On the presence of diversity from the very beginning see S. Schulz, 'Die Anfänge urchristlicher Verkündigung. Zur Traditions- und Theologiegeschichte der ältesten Christenheit' in *Die Mitte des Neuen Testaments* (see n. 2), pp. 254-271.

choices. I leave aside the very brief confessions like 'Jesus is Lord' as lacking content. The creed most usually favoured by those who adopted this approach was that summary which Paul handed on to the Corinthians:

> For I delivered to you as of first importance what I also received, that Christ died for our sins in accordance with the scriptures, that he was buried, that he was raised on the third day in accordance with the scriptures, and that he appeared to Cephas, then to the twelve (1 Cor. 15.3-5).

Alternatively the Philippian hymn (2.6-11) could be advanced or the summary of Peter's sermon to Cornelius (Acts 10.34-43) or what appears to be the content of Paul's first preaching to the Thessalonians:

> You must turn from idols to serve the living and true God and wait for his son from heaven, whom he raised from the dead, Jesus who delivers us from the wrath to come (1 Thess. 1.9f.).

Curiously what I take to be the only definition of Christianity in the New Testament was never suggested:

> Religion (and in its context that is not a reference to religion in general but to Christianity) that is pure and undefiled before God and the Father is this: to visit orphans and widows in their affliction, and to keep oneself unstained from the world (James 1.27).

These brief creeds are all very different. They do not all even refer to the death of Jesus. None of them mentions God as creator. Only the summary of Peter's speech to Cornelius introduces the Holy Spirit. Only the verse from James introduces the need for some kind of moral behaviour on the part of Christians. They are then all very truncated expressions of Christianity.

(5) In view of the failure to extract from Scripture any brief creed which fully represented primitive Christianity it might be more helpful if we attempted to draw up one for ourselves which would take account of the areas neglected in those we have examined. I shall consider two attempts. The first, that which C. H. Dodd framed as representing the preaching of the primitive church as it could be learnt from Acts with corrobo-

ration from the Pauline letters. Dodd did not intend this to represent the central message of the New Testament but from time to time others seemed to have taken it in that way. Dodd offered six points:

1. The prophecies of the Old Testament have now been fulfilled.
2. This has happened in the ministry, death and resurrection of Jesus.
3. He has now been exalted to God's right hand as Messiah and Lord.
4. This belief has been confirmed by the gift of the Holy Spirit.
5. Jesus will return to bring God's purposes to their consummation.
6. Meanwhile men have an opportunity to repent and to receive forgiveness and the gift of the Holy Spirit.[11]

Most of the language in this summary is biblical or closely related to the Bible. Its attractiveness lies in that and also in the feeling that in it we come close to the earliest gospel as the first apostles proclaimed it and thus near to Christ. The earliest as the purest?

Before we leave it I would draw your attention to one significant feature within it and one problem raised by it. The feature is the explicit reference to the Old Testament, admittedly present also in 1 Cor. 15.3-5. For the moment we note this; we shall return to it later. The problem relates to the faith of the summariser. Dodd was not very keen on seeing the parousia as a part of true Christianity but he included it in the summary because it was important for the first Christians. Has then the central message to be in accord with what we take to

[11]C. H. Dodd, *The Apostolic Preaching and its Developments*, Hodder and Stoughton, London, 1944, pp. 21ff. I have quoted the summary as given in G. B. Caird, *The Apostolic Age*, Duckworth, London, 1955, pp. 37f.

be the essence of present Christian faith or with the faith of the primitive church?

(6) In the winter of 1899-1900 Harnack gave public lectures in the University of Berlin on the nature of Christianity. He extracted what he took to be its essence from the teaching of Jesus and expressed it in three sentences which became the section headings in his outline of that teaching:

i. The kingdom of God and its coming.
ii. God the Father and the infinite value of the human soul.
iii. The higher righteousness and the commandment of love.[12]

Unlike many of his fellow liberal theologians Harnack did not reject Paul.[13] He began with the picture of Jesus and argued that Paul had followed Jesus in his own writing. What conservative, and indeed many other Christians, would term the essential Paul just disappeared from his picture of Paul. Thus his summary of Jesus' teaching became in effect his summary of the message of the New Testament. He acknowledged the apocalyptic element in the teaching of Jesus but regarded it as occasioned by the period in which Jesus lived and not as essential to it. He believed he had therefore been able to unleash the eternal message of Jesus from its contemporary trappings and to restate it. A comparison of his summary with that of Dodd shows that unlike Dodd's it is framed in non-biblical terms and is consciously designed to express the central message of the New Testament in the terms of Harnack's own generation and culture. This raises a question to which we shall return, but before leaving Harnack it is wise to remember that like Luther but unlike Dodd he had a great public hearing.

(7) We turn finally to J. D. G. Dunn who alone of those we have considered has set out deliberately to define the central

---

[12]A. Harnack, *What is Christianity* (E.T. by T. B. Saunders), Ernest Benn, London, 1958.
[13]Op. cit., 128ff.

message of the New Testament. Recognising the variety of material it contains he concludes his book *Unity and Diversity in the New Testament* by setting out what he terms its 'unifying strand' or 'integrating centre':[14]

> That unifying element was the unity between the historical Jesus and the exalted Christ, that is to say, the conviction that the wandering charismatic preacher from Nazareth had ministered, died and been raised from the dead to bring God and man finally together, the recognition that the divine power through which they now worshipped and were encountered and accepted by God was one and the same person, Jesus, the man, the Christ, the Son of God, the Lord, the life-giving Spirit.[15]

We note here that the unity of the New Testament is defined in terms of a modern theological issue, the relation of the historical Jesus and the exalted Christ.[16] No one denies that this issue has bulked large in recent scholarly work but it would hardly have been acceptable as a unifying theme at the time of the Reformation and I suspect will not be a hundred, perhaps not even twenty, years from now.

III

We now turn to some of the issues which have been appearing in one or other of these statements of the central message. I intend to raise a number of questions which seem in the light of the attempts we have examined to require an answer before the formulation of the central message is itself attacked. For lack of time I cannot treat two major fields of concern: Is there a canon within the canon? Is there a New Testament theology or are there a number of such theologies?

(1) There is one major area on which it is necessary to touch even if it is impossible to deal satisfactorily with it: In how far

---

[14]S.C.M., London, 1977, p. 369; cf. p. 376.

[15]Op. cit. p. 369; cf. p. 376.

[16]Cf. S. Neil, *Jesus through Many Eyes*, Fortress, Philadelphia, 1976, p. 180, 'There is a real continuity between the words of Jesus and the words about Jesus'.

is the answer we give dictated by the view of the nature of the New Testament with which we commence? We might take it to be a verbally and infallibly inspired series of propositions. Summaries of documents of this type are common and select the most important propositions from which the others can be derived. Alternatively the New Testament might be regarded as a set of reactions or responses to the needs of particular situations. From the way someone behaves in differing situations we learn quite a lot about them and sum them up in a phrase or word. So the New Testament might be summed up in a brief statement or an idea or a symbol. If we toss a stone into a pond we set up a series of ever-widening ripples. The writings of the New Testament could be regarded as these ripples with Jesus as the stone. Since as the ripples spread they are affected by the wind and drifting debris we would need to take a ripple as near as possible to the point where the stone was thrown, i.e. an early creed would seem most satisfactory. There are many other possible views of the New Testament but we neither need to enumerate or evaluate them. My point is that before we can begin to answer the problem which is the subject of this lecture we need to be clear in our own minds what we take the New Testament to be. I go on now to raise some less fundamental issues.[17]

(2) What areas of the content of the New Testament should any statement of its central message cover? If we look at the historic creeds of the church they contain both historical material, 'suffered under Pontius Pilate' and propositional material, 'God of God; Light of Light'. But they do not contain ethical or experiential material. If we recall the answers to our problem at which we have already looked most of them also

---

[17]My own views will be found in *From Text to Sermon*, 2nd edn. T. & T. Clark, Edinburgh 1988, chapter 1 and in 'Scripture, Tradition and the Canon of the New Testament', *Bulletin John Rylands University Library Manchester*, 61 (1979), pp. 258-289, within pp. 14ff.

lacked these two areas. Is there not a need to include statements of the type 'Love your neighbour as yourself' and 'you must be born again'? To put this another way: all the statements at which we have looked were cast in the indicative mood; are statements in the imperative mood not also necessary? If someone alleges that statements require to be cast in the indicative then this raises the question whether what we are really after can in fact be framed as a statement.

(3) Are we attempting to express what is central to the New Testament or what is central to the Christianity of the first century? If the latter we might have to delete from consideration any books of the New Testament written outside that period and to include any others, or any other evidence of whatever type, coming from within that period. That however is in a way a minor matter. The significance of the question can be seen when we realise that the importance of a belief or practice to the early church may not be proportional to the amount of material about it in the New Testament. Christology of some kind features on its every page but outside the Gospels we rarely find direct teaching about God. The first Christians were Jews and probably did not need much of such teaching. In addition views that at one time were important in primitive Christianity may later have been played down. We do not learn from Acts the extent of the bitterness of the controversy about the admission of Gentiles to the church. Whatever diversity we discover within the New Testament is probably only a reflection of the wider diversity within first century Christianity. Many streams of thought have been detected:[18] a Jewish Christianity, perhaps to be associated with Q, a Pauline, a Johannine receptive of many ideas from Hellenism. Perhaps there was also a stream which ran off into the developed gnostic

---

[18]Pokorný, op. cit., 68, 80, while not doubting the existence of different christological strands doubts whether they can today be easily disentangled from one another. E.T., pp. 88, 105.

systems of the second century. These streams did not all necessarily accept one another as valid manifestations of the Faith. Extreme Jewish Christians did not accept Paul; nor did the Johannine stream if it is held to include Revelation for it gives only twelve gates into heaven, one for each of the Twelve and none for Paul. If we decide to seek a centre to first century Christianity rather than to the New Testament we must also answer the question as to the date at which we should seek that centre. The centre might have been formulated very differently in AD 50 and AD 100. One last problem in this area: our primary source for our understanding of the first century is the New Testament; if there are already difficulties about determining its centre will there be not even more about determining that of which it only partially reports?

(4) Is the statement, to employ mathematical terms, to be the HCF or the LCD of the content of the various writings of the New Testament? To put this another way: have we to disentangle a definition which is found in or underlies every writing or have we to frame a definition which includes every important statement made in any one of the writings? Note the use of the word 'important' here. Whatever views we may have on the superiority of one author to another in the New Testament there is no doubt that within any one writer there are relatively more and less important passages. That Jesus died on the cross is much more important than that he performed a particular healing in Capernaum rather than Jericho. Clearly judgments can vary as to what is important; there are commentaries on Romans which peter out after 12.8[19] and on Galatians after 4.11[20] as if what follows did not matter. So how does one decide what is important? The presuppositions with which we

---

[19]E.g. A. Nygren, *Commentary on Romans* (E.T. by C. C. Rasmussen), S.C.M., London 1952.

[20]E.g. G. Ebeling, *Die Wahrheit des Evangeliums*, J. C. B. Mohr (Paul Siebeck), Tübingen, 1981.

commence will determine what we end up with. Our personal view of the nature of Christianity may determine what we consider important in the New Testament. If we take orthopraxis to be relatively unimportant compared with orthodoxy we shall write off the end of Romans and Galatians. But how do we determine what is important? The argument is bound to be to a certain extent circular. To deal with this it has been suggested that there are a number of relational centres like the incarnation or the Kingdom of God to which everything else may be connected;[21] but the selection of these centres would not go undisputed. Dodd and Harnack would not have agreed on what they were.

(5) In what terms should the statement be expressed? Dodd and Harnack chose very different types of words; Dodd selected his mainly from the New Testament itself, Harnack from current religious discussion. It might seem that we would answer the implied question solely in terms of our theological position. Of that I am not sure. Other factors may enter. The author of Colossians appears to have taken up gnostic, i.e. non-biblical, terminology current in his community to express what he thought was a basic theological position. If our supposed summary statement is intended for the use of non-Christians that might be the better approach. And that raises another question to which we shall return: for whom is the statement designed? As we are beginning to see the questions which we need to face are not wholly unrelated to one another and too hasty an answer to one may commit us to answers to others before we have reached and considered them.

(6) Is the statement intended to be one which faithfully describes what a first century Christian might have answered

[21]Cf. E. Flesseman-van Leer (ed.), *The Bible: Its Authority and Interpretation in the Ecumenical Movement*, Faith and Order Paper No. 99, World Council of Churches, Geneva, 1980, pp. 50f.

or is it to be one acceptable to contemporary theological opinion, to say nothing of non-theological opinion. If we decide it should be acceptable to a first century Christian we need to specify which. Would Paul have agreed with a summary drawn up by Luke or John, to say nothing of James? The issue here about the first century and today is not quite the same as, but is not unconnected to, the question whether in interpreting a text we seek the meaning 'then' or the meaning 'now'. Another way of putting it is to ask whether our statement is to be one intended to satisfy an academic examining board or one to be used in explaining Christianity to a church group? Both Luther and Harnack believed that their very different answers had contemporary relevance. An illustration will point up the issue and relate it to some of the other questions. Within the New Testament the parousia occupies a very prominent position; it does not do so in many modern theologies. Ought it to be included in any statement of the central message? If we omit it our summary will certainly not be acceptable in the southern United States. If we include it some will say that we are burdening ourselves unnecessarily.

(7) You will have observed that in some of the suggested summary statements the Old Testament has featured either directly or indirectly. Ought it to be there? This is an equivalent question to that which asks whether a New Testament theology can exist independently of the Old Testament. Marcion's summary of the New Testament would certainly not have contained any reference to the Old Testament. Our answers here will depend on the degree to which we see the New Testament as dependent on the old.

(8) This leads to yet another question. In the strict sense the Old Testament has no christology; only a theology. Almost all, if not all, the summary statements at which we looked were *christo*logically oriented rather than *theo*logically. It was natural that Christian Jews should express the centre of their faith

in christological terms. This was what was new. They still
believed in the same God as they had always believed in, but
they now understood him in a new way through Jesus. Thus
they naturally emphasised christology. When the message was
taken to the hellenistic world it was unusual to find atheists;
again what was required was a modification of the Gentile's
view of his god or gods in the light of his encounter with Christ.
Hence all the brief statements and creeds in the New Testament are centred on Christ and God is hardly mentioned. If we
are to express fairly the intention of the New Testament ought
we not then to introduce into our central message some
mention of God? To take a particular example. It was unnecessary to stress in the New Testament a supernatural origin to
the world for almost no one doubted that it was supernaturally
created in some way. This belief was part and parcel of
unexpressed New Testament faith. Should it appear in our
summary?

(9) Must every expression of the central message be set in
terms dictated by the culture in which it is drawn up or is there
an eternally valid core which can be expressed in eternally valid
words? Since some New Testament statements are more
important than others it is relatively easy to think of a distinction existing between core and periphery or between constants
and variables.[22] But if we allow that there is a core can this be
put into invariant words which will never need to be changed?
Clearly those who thought the kerygma could be expressed in
one of the New Testament's own brief creeds were unworried
by any doubts about this. They recognised neither the cultural
conditioning of every part of Scripture nor their own cultural
conditioning. Returning briefly to the last point: the New
Testament creeds exhibit their cultural conditioning by the

---

[22]Cf. D. A. Hagner, 'Biblical theology and preaching', *Exp. Times*, 96 (1984/5), pp. 137-
141.

absence of any need to express directly a belief in God; our culture may require us deliberately to draw this out because today so many in Western Europe are practical atheists, whatever the opinion polls may reveal about their supposed belief in God.

(10) This leads to another most important question. If a brief central message is required for whom is it being drafted? Luther and Harnack had the world at large in their sights; Dodd and Dunn had, or have, their colleagues and students. The nature of the audience will obviously determine the type of language, academic, ecclesiological or everyday, to be used in its compilation. An allied question to that of the prospective audience is the purpose for which the brief statement is intended? Some academics might answer in the terms 'mountains exist to be climbed'. Ecclesiastical politicians might wish a statement so that they can use it to check on the views of supposed 'heretics'. Yet others might desire one in order to form a basis for the uniting of two denominations. In such cases it often turns out to be so inexact as to be almost meaningless or ambiguous words are employed so that everyone will be satisfied. Any simple statement may indeed conceal more than it reveals. If it is designed for church use there is still an important question to be settled: is it intended for internal use within the church or for apologetic and missionary use outside it? These issues bring us back to a previous question: if the constituency for which it is intended does not have the firm and accepted belief in the existence of God which was to be found in the first century world will something of this nature not need to be expressed and the statement become theological in tone rather than christological?

(11) As we have been thinking about these questions you may have been checking out in your mind the answers you would give, or you may have been moved to ask a more fundamental question. Is a verbal statement in fact possible?

Would we not be better to give up the idea and approach the matter in some other way. Perhaps by using the term 'message' I gave our inquiry the wrong orientation from the beginning. The parts of the New Testament may be so linked together that they cannot be isolated and some selected as more important than others. Just as Paul rebuked the Corinthians for desiring positions of prominence within their community by reminding them that they were members of the one Body so the parts of the New Testament may be linked to one another as in an organism and require the support of one another.[23] To isolate certain elements in a brief summary may be to destroy the unity of the whole. It may be then that we ought be looking for a central drive or thrust rather than a statement.

Such a drive or thrust need not necessarily be expressed in strictly verbal terms. This is what Luther had in mind when he isolated as the central drive what preached Christ. Yet this as we have seen turned out to be so vague that Luther had to go on and define it more precisely in terms of justification by faith. Another approach along these general lines might be to say that a sign or symbol would be the best expression of the centre of the New Testament. Clearly the sign would have to be something like a cross. Last year I was in Seoul, S. Korea, and from a high-rise building it was possible to pick out the churches by their illuminated crosses. The power of that symbol in a pagan city cannot be disregarded. Yet those who mounted those crosses on their buildings would probably be among the first to say that of themselves they were insufficient and were only intended to guide people inside where they would receive a verbal message. The New Testament is verbal and it is doubtful if we can entirely escape stating in words what is central to it.

[23]Cf. Watson (see n. 6).

Perhaps then instead of a sign we might select an idea, necessarily verbally expressed, which would give the key to the whole. The liberal theologians of last century selected the kingdom of God, conservative evangelicals might pick 'born again', 'reconciliation'[24] would be popular in a western democracy and 'liberation' in the third world. The 'man for others' had its brief vogue. None of these means much without considerably further expansion. To the western world kingly rule is almost unknown, Nicodemus had great difficulty in grasping what rebirth was, who is being reconciled in reconciliation (an employer and a trade union being led to a compromise with which neither is fully satisfied?) from what are people being liberated in liberation? Is the Son of God just a *man* for others?

One further way of escaping this verbal tangle may be to look for the unity of the New Testament in the recipients of the kerygma rather than in a form of words. Any statement of the central message will be mythological in character and unsuitable to the situation of the contemporary world. To insist on words is to tear apart the act of thinking from the act of living.[25] An existentialist translation of the words thus becomes a necessity, and for some theologians this means they must be expressed in anthropological rather than theological terms. The New Testament offers us a genuine understanding of ourselves. This understanding is produced in varying degrees by its different writings but principally by those of Paul and John. Bultmann, for whom this might have been a possible approach if we had been able to ask him about it, in outlining Paul's theology breaks it up not according to the normal christological, pneumatological and ecclesiological divisions

[24]E.g. P. Stuhlmacher, *Vom Verstehen des Neuen Testaments: Eine Hermeneutik*, Vandenhoeck & Ruprecht, Göttingen, 1979, pp. 225ff.

[25]Cf. R. Bultmann, *Theology of the New Testament*, S.C.M., London, 1952, 1955, Vol. II, pp. 250f.

but in relation to man before and after faith. What unifies the writings of the New Testament may then be the self-understanding they produce in those who hear the kerygma in faith. Yet even if this be granted it does not seem that we escape our problem for if man's self-understanding is to be communicated it needs to be expressed verbally. Most of our questions would then still remain.

(12) It is curious but significant how little the Gospels have entered into this discussion. They comprise more than 45 per cent of the New Testament and if Acts is added as further narrative more than 58 per cent. The early church had presumably good reasons for including such narratives. But can narrative be summarised? Is not an essential element lost in the very attempt. Those who have read the summaries of novels that have been produced from time to time by the Readers' Digest or by educational (?) publishers for the benefit of children preparing for examinations can have no doubt how much the summary loses. Almost all the statements we have considered have concentrated on the birth, death and resurrection of Jesus. Harnack may have drawn on the life of Jesus but it was only in order to produce propositional statements. The sermon of Peter in Acts 10 included a brief reference to Jesus' activities during his ministry but the author of Acts did not need to give more for his readers already had his Gospel in their hands with its much fuller account.

We are predisposed by the way we conduct our academic work to value propositional statements above narrative. Yet may the question not be raised as to the indispensability of narrative to Christianity. If this is answered affirmatively where are we to find a place for narrative in a central message if narrative loses a great part of its value in being summarised? The first Christians obviously found simple credal statements insufficient. Letters treating particular issues needed to be written; then the Gospels were composed. The early Christians must have reasoned at least in part like this: if we say Jesus healed, we need stories of how he actually healed; if we say he loved sinners, we need stories of how he loved particular people; and so on. From the variety of incidents recorded much more is learnt than from any simple affirmation that he healed and loved. Indeed to deny this would be tantamount to denying a major section of the canon.

But would one Gospel not be sufficient? Why four? If we only had one we would lose a considerable number of incidents and therefore of variety. Would a harmony like Tatian's *Diatessaron* not overcome this difficulty? No facts would be lost. But even if at one stage and perhaps still in the popular mind the Gospels are miniature biographies no scholar today would allow that each does not also carry an interpretation of what is reported, and this applies as much to the individual synoptic Gospels as to the Fourth. A harmony would carry an interpretation of its own not necessarily reflecting the interpretation of any one of our four Gospels but certainly reflecting the interpretation of its compiler. Moreover if as I argued earlier variety within the New Testament is important this is surely also true of the four Gospels and for the same reason. We need four narratives of Jesus not simply that we may have a greater variety of material but so that we may see that no one interpretation of any particular incident or of Jesus himself is absolute. If Jesus is to be easily related to our situation either as the historical Jesus or the preached Christ then variety of interpretation is essential.

This brings us to the crux of our problem. The existence of the Gospels makes any central message a shadowy substitute for the real thing. If we think back a little to the reasons offered for the value of the diversity of the New Testament we will recollect that it was its very diversity which enabled it to be used in our culture and situations. If we reduce it to a set of statements, a simple drive or a core then we shall always have difficulty in applying it. (This may not be a problem if we are concerned only with discovering some centre for academic purposes). It is important then to retain both the diversity of ethical situation and response in the letters and to retain the variety of outlook in the four Gospels. If we attempt to formulate a central message may we not be robbing the New Testament of something which is essential to it and to our use of it?

There with only one or two further remarks I must stop. I acknowledge that from time to time the church needs to define what it believes and in so far as it sees the New Testament as either the primary source for its belief or normative for it it will draw up brief statements of its central message. These may be necessary both to rebut heresy and to affirm truth, especially perhaps when churches are in discussion with one another. All such statements will be time-conditioned and will repeatedly require renewal and replacement. There is no neutral statement which will last for ever. Even academics as they write New Testament theologies and answer the questions of their students are forced from generation to generation to change what they say. In the end it is because of the cultural conditioning of any statement, the need for a precise definition of the situation for which it is required and the narrative nature of the Gospels that I have refrained from offering you the form I think it ought to take.

Whenever I preach I endeavour to bring that to which the New Testament witnesses before my hearers. This Sunday's sermon and next Sunday's will be very different because I start from different passages of Scripture and face different issues. Anyone who recorded all I said would find contradictions for there is no simple core message to be repeated in parrot fashion from Sunday to Sunday but a continuing re-expression of that to which the New Testament itself is faithful. I end with a couple of examples drawn from the New Testament. The first comes from Paul when he was attempting to persuade the Corinthians to contribute more generously to the needs of the saints in Jerusalem. Into the middle of a number of more or less prudential arguments he threw in one which not only destroyed all his careful prudence but, more importantly, restated the doctrine of the incarnation in a vivid and exceptionally relevant way:

> For you know the grace of our Lord Jesus Christ, that though he was rich, yet for your sake he became poor, so that by his poverty you might become rich (2 Cor. 8.9).

In AD 56 in Corinth that was probably the central message of the New Testament, but it was probably not that for AD 57 when chapters ten to thirteen of 2 Corinthians were being written. The second example is drawn from the First Letter of John. Dealing with an actual schism, or the possibility of one, in which those with whom he disagreed were stressing spiritual experience, knowing God, rather than loving behaviour the author wrote:

> He who does not love does not know God; for God is love (4.8).

That was the central message in Asia at the end of the first century. Again it might not be the way we would put it.

5

EXORCISM IN THE NEW TESTAMENT AND TODAY

Belief in demons and the practice of exorcism is not especially Christian. It was known in the ancient world outside Christianity and evidence for this exists even within the New Testament itself. When the Pharisees accused Jesus of casting out demons by Beelzebul the prince of demons, he answered them by asking 'And if I cast out demons by Beelzebul, by whom do your sons cast them out?' (Matt. 12.27). In another story the disciple John tells Jesus that he forbade a man who was casting out demons in Jesus' name to continue to do so because he was not a disciple; there is no surprise on John's part that the man cast out demons, but only surprise that he uses Jesus' name; this implies that John was accustomed to the practice of exorcism (Mark 9.38f.; cf. Acts 19.33ff.).

There is also plenty of evidence outside the New Testament in non-Christian writings for the practice. Two examples will suffice. Josephus, the Jewish historian, tells the story of an exorcism that took place in his own time (the first century A.D.).

> And this kind of cure is of very great power among us to this day, for I have seen a certain Eleazar, a countryman of mine, in the presence of Vespasian, his sons, tribunes and a number of other soldiers, free men possessed by demons, and this was the manner of the cure; he put to the nose of the possessed man a ring which had under its seal one of the roots prescribed by Solomon, and then, as the man smelled it, drew out the demon through his nostrils, and, when the man at once fell down, adjured the demon never to come back into him, speaking Solomon's name and reciting the incantations which he had composed.

Then, wishing to convince the bystanders and prove to them that he had this power, Eleazar placed a cup or foot-basin full of water a little way off and commanded the demon, as it went out of the man, to overturn it and make known to the spectators that he had left the man. (*Ant* VIII. 45-48).[1]

Non-Jewish evidence for the practice is found in Philostratus' *The Life of Apollonius* where he tells of Apollonius:

(One day Apollonius was interrupted by a young man so that he could not be heard). Apollonius looked up at him and said: 'It is not yourself that perpetrates this insult, but the demon who drives you on without your knowing it.' And in fact the youth was, without knowing it, possessed by a devil; for he would laugh at things that no one else laughed at, and then he would fall to weeping for no reason at all, and he would talk and sing to himself. Now when Apollonius gazed on him, the ghost in him began to utter cries of fear and rage, such as one hears from people who are being branded or racked; and the ghost swore that he would leave the young man alone and never take possession of any man again. But Apollonius addressed him with anger, as a master might a shifty, rascally and shameless slave and so on, and he ordered him to quit the young man and show by a visible sign that he had done so. 'I will throw down yonder statue', said the devil, and pointed to one of the images which was in the king's portico, for there it was that the scene took place. But when the statue began by moving gently, and then fell down, it would defy anyone to describe the hubbub which arose thereat and the way they clapped their hands with wonder.[2]

These are only two of the many references in ancient literature.[3]

Exorcism only exists where there is a belief in demons. A demon is an evil personal being subordinate to the supreme

---

[1]Loeb translation. In Jewish tradition Solomon was believed to have been an exorcist and his name was regularly used in exorcisms. See *Testament of Solomon* (ed. C. C. McCown, Untersuchungen zum N.T. 9; Liepzig, 1922).

[2]IV. 20 (Loeb translation).

[3]For further examples and discussion see T. K. Oesterreich *Possession: Demonical and Other* (E.T. by D. Ibberson; London, 1930), J. Hull *Hellenistic Magic and the Synoptic Tradition* (London, 1974), C. Bonner 'The Technique of Exorcism' *HTR* 36 (1943) 39-49. The latter identifies three things which the demon was normally forced to do in the ancient exorcism: (1) to speak in answer to the exorcist, (2) to disclose his name or nature, (3) to give visible proof of his departure from the man he possessed.

evil personal being, Satan or the Devil. The belief in demons
was widespread in the ancient world, and is of course widespread today in many primitive cultures. The demon is supposed to live in, or possess the man who is afflicted by him.
There can also be a belief in beneficial spirits who inspire men
to good or heroic activities, but these do not require to be
exorcised.

Turning to the New Testament we find that most of the
stories of exorcism by Jesus are in the Gospel of Mark.
Matthew and Luke repeat the stories of Mark, but do not add
greatly to their number. Often they abbreviate them and
sometimes they omit them. John is reticent about demons. It
is not only that Mark narrates exorcism, but at a number of
points in his Gospel he deliberately draws attention to the
practice. From time to time he inserts little summaries describing the activities of Jesus. In one of these he writes:

> And whenever the unclean spirits beheld him, they fell down before him
> and cried out, 'You are the Son of God'. And he strictly ordered them
> not to make him known. (Mark 3.11f.).

Why does Mark draw attention to the exorcisms? It may be
said that he does so because they happened. There is no reason
to doubt that they did. Many people have doubts about some
of the things which Jesus did e.g., walking on the water, feeding
the five thousand. Few people doubt that he exorcised, for, as
we have seen, it was a normal practice in his own day. But it was
so unremarkable a feature of his own day that Mark cannot just
have repeated the stories because they happened, but because
he saw some special significance in them. What was this? (1)
As victories over demons they represent Jesus' victory over evil
as a whole, i.e., his victory over Satan. (2) In each of the stories
that Mark records, and this appears also in his summary of
Jesus' activity as exorcist (see above) the demon confesses Jesus:
in the summary he says that Jesus is the Son of God; cf. 1.24;
5.7. Mark is giving the witness of the supernatural world, even

if it is the evil supernatural world, to the true nature of Jesus. (3) In the story of the boy (9. 14-29) whom the disciples could not heal when Jesus was away from them on the Mount of Transfiguration, Jesus after healing him ends by saying to the disciples 'This kind cannot be driven out by anything but prayer' (9.29). The story instructs the disciples how they are to exorcise.

Mark also stresses that the disciples are sent by Jesus to practice exorcism. When the twelve are chosen it is so that they may be 'with him, and be sent out to preach and have authority to cast out demons' (3. 14f. cf. 6.7, 13). In the early church we know that Christians practised exorcism (Acts 16. 16-18).

They continued the practice beyond the New Testament period. There is an account in the apocryphal 'Acts of Peter' written in the second century:

Then Peter turned to the crowd who stood by him, and saw in the crowd a man half laughing, in whom was a most wicked demon. And Peter said to him, 'Whoever you are, that laughed, show yourself openly to all who stand by.' And hearing this the young man ran into the courtyard of the house, and he shouted aloud and threw himself against the wall and said, 'Peter, there is a huge contest between (p. 59) Simon and the dog which you sent; for Simon says to the dog, 'Say that I am not here' — but the dog says more to him than the message you gave; and when he has finished the mysterious work which you gave him, he shall die at your feet.' But Peter said, 'You too, then, whatever demon you may be, in the name of our Lord Jesus Christ, come out of the young man and do him no harm; (and) show yourself to all who stand by!' And hearing this he left the young man; and he caught hold of a great marble statue, which stood in the courtyard of the house and kicked it to pieces.[4]

In all these exorcisms the exorcist takes up a position of authority, either the authority is his own as in the case of Jesus, or it is derived from Jesus or God (in so far as the exorcism is Christian), and he commands the demon to come out, but he

---

[4]*Acts of Peter* 4.11 in *New Testament Apocrypha* (ed. Hennecke-Schneelmecher-Wilson) vol. II, p. 293f.

does not offer forgiveness of sin. Possession by a demon may
be evil, but it is not treated as sinful. The victim is not offered
forgiveness, but the expulsion of his demon. There are, of
course, different types of evil. We commonly make a distinction between the evil that is in an earthquake or in a disease and
the evil that lies in personal sin. The evil relating to possession
seems to lie in the area of the former. But is it not said that Judas
is possessed by a devil and is this not why he betrayed Jesus? If
we look carefully, we see that it is not said that Judas was
possessed by a demon, but that Satan entered Judas (Luke
22.3; John 13.27). It is no subordinate or lesser demon, but the
Devil himself who takes possession of Judas. His behaviour is
not explained in terms of demonic possession, but of a unique
satanic possession.

It is important to note also that it is only in Luke and John
that Judas' action is attributed to Satan; in the earlier Gospel
of Mark Satan does not appear. In fact Satan, the Devil, is
largely unknown in the Old Testament; as an evil being
opposed to God he entered Judaism from the religion of Iran
in the centuries just before Jesus and it is only in the first
century A.D. that we really encounter him as the one who
tempts to sin. Thus in the first century demons could easily be
conceived as a source of evil without being necessarily associated with sin. In line with this it is not surprising to find Jesus
speaking to the storm (Mk. 4.39) with the same command he
uses to a demon (1.29).

What has this to do with us? We do not live in a world in
which supernatural forces of evil, whether personal or not, are
regarded as having an influence on what happened. If an
earthquake takes place we know that it is caused by some
disturbance in the lower crusts of the earth's surface. If
someone takes ill we attribute it to an infection, the failure to
observe rules of health, or to some other outward and physical
or inward and psychical cause, but we do not attribute illness

to demons. We assume that all the things which happen around us have an ordinary cause which, if we had enough time and energy, we would be able to understand and explain. Nature is a uniform system and whatever happens happens because of some previous event. Yet we also realise that there are vast areas of the world where people still believe in demons and we regularly refer to these areas as the more primitive areas. We have also seen within our own western civilisation accounts of exorcism, some of which have been frightening. What are we to make of them? If on the one hand the Bible talks about demons and possessed people, and if Jesus practised exorcism and yet we as citizens of the twentieth century have no place in our daily lives for demonic influence, how are we to resolve this conflict?

Let us begin with the use of the exorcism stories in preaching. One way in which the conflict has been resolved has been to take the stories and make them mean something other than what they do mean. Instead of thinking of literal demonic possession we substitute something which we can more easily understand and grapple with, e.g., the demon of Nazi nationalism or the demon of drink, sex or money. Undoubtedly Nazism and the abuse of drink, sex and wealth are all evil, but they are not demons in the way in which these were thought of in the first century. The attitude we take up towards them at other times shows that we regard them as sinful rather than evil in the way an earthquake or sickness is evil. The demon was exorcised, that is to say, he was ordered to come out of the man. No one addressed the German nation in this kind of way and ordered the Nazi demon to come out from it; instead men attempted to deal with what was wrong by force of arms; demons, if they are spiritual forces of evil, cannot be overcome by bombs. No one faced with an alcoholic attempts to expel a demon from him, but tries instead by various ways to persuade him to allow himself to be dried out. Nazism and alcohol are not supernatural personal demons, but natural things and we deal with them by using natural methods.

People in industrialised Western civilisation do not in their normal lives believe in demons. Some may wish to query this, and say that while in ordinary life they do not accept the existence of demons yet they reserve an area for them in the field of religion, on the grounds that Jesus believed in demons. It may be possible to defend a position like this, but it would entail a long and difficult argument to maintain that whereas the ordinary laws of nature hold in the whole of secular life there is a special area of religion in which they do not hold. It seems easier to accept that the same laws should govern the whole of life — and this was accepted in the first century. The man of that time did not see universal laws as governing nature and, therefore, did not see demonic possession as an exception to them. He saw all nature, including sickness, as governed directly by God or the gods. Thus he believed in astrology; the stars, because they were inhabited by deities, controlled what happened in daily life. He believed in magic; by the performance of certain rites he could influence what was happening in the world around him. He believed that God and the gods acted directly to make it rain whenever it rained and that God made the sun rise every day by his direct intervention. Within a world of belief like this acceptance of demonic possession was not extraordinary but normal. For us to believe in it is to believe in the extraordinary; for the man of the first century it was just another part of his ordinary daily life.

But what about Jesus' belief in demon possession? Again, it is a difficult and involved argument if we give it the full treatment. If the incarnation of Jesus was real, then he must have been a man of his own time, believing the same things as ordinary people did. On earth he had no exceptional access to knowledge other than that which other people had. So like the remainder of men in those days he believed that when it rained it was because God had made it rain. We explain rain through meteorological science; we may not always be able to predict accurately when rain will come, but we believe that some day this will be achieved; the weather is wholly subject to natural laws and is not conceived as deriving from God's direct activity or a demon's. If Jesus had lived today, this is the kind of belief he would have had, but living in his own day, belief in demons was part and parcel of the way a real man looked at the world around him, and Jesus did not contract out of being a real man.

It is important to point out that to disbelieve in demon possession does not necessarily imply a disbelief in either the existence of evil or of a personal power of evil. Belief in the devil does not entail belief in demons. Beliefs in that area are related to the problem of the origin and nature of evil and go far beyond the scope of this paper.

But if we want to believe in demons we encounter a further difficulty. Most psychiatrists today would say that what we term demonic possession can be explained in psychological terms.[5] In order to understand those who appear to be possessed, we do not need to introduce the hypothesis of the demon, but we need operate only in terms of the laws of the mind. There are still people who if they had lived in an earlier age would have been described as demon-possessed. Outwardly the sickness appears to be the same, but the explanation for it has changed. In many parts of Ireland years ago when a cow stopped giving milk its owner would assume that someone had put the evil eye on it, i.e., had bewitched it. Today he would call in a vet to find out what was wrong. Cows may still dry up but we look for an explanation in terms of the laws of

[5]Michael Wilson, 'Exorcism', *Exp. T.* 86 (1974/5) 291-5, who is both physician and minister, has some discussion of the medical aspects.

nature rather than in terms of the supernatural. In the story of
Mark 9. 14-29 the child's sickness is attributed to demon
possession. When the story is retold in Matthew 17. 14-21 the
boy is described as an epileptic. In the ancient world epilepsy
was often ascribed to demon possession. Today we treat
epilepsy as a natural illness and it can be controlled by medical
means, even if the sufferer cannot always be fully cured.
Similarly 'natural' explanations would be given today for many
other sicknesses which in the ancient world were attributed to
evil spirits.

But is there not a recrudescence today of belief in demon
possession? Cases are regularly reported in the newspaper. In
the Church of England the ancient rite of exorcism has been
revived and there are priests who practise it, both in relation to
demon-possessed people and to houses or property affected by
ghosts. If it is out of harmony with the way in which we mostly
live our lives, in which we expect things to proceed from day
to day in a natural law-abiding way, how do we account for this
recrudescence?

We will not be surprised by it once we realise it is part of a
much wider phenomenon. There has been a revival in recent
years of belief in the irrational. Many magazines and newspa-
pers today carry an astrological column; astrology and demon
possession were part of the same culture in the ancient world.
There is also today a greater interest in magic and witchcraft.
People are as superstitious as ever they were. There is a
tremendous interest in the phenomena of parapsychology,
though these phenomena are not necessarily on the same level
as superstition, astrology and magic, but the very keen interest
taken in them by ordinary people, with what might almost be
described as a desire to believe, is another indication of interest
in the irrational. This is again all part of a reaction against the
ordered rule of daily life which for many people has become
boring, regimented and unpleasant. They want to escape the

rat race in which personality cannot develop. Some young people use drugs, others opt out of the normal habits of society. Outbursts of irrational violence from football supporters are part of the same reaction. All this irrationality is much more like life in the first century than life as it went on half a century ago. There is a partial breakdown in the belief in an ordered way of existence. This may only be a temporary matter. We cannot see how far it is going to go, nor how long it will last. In the first century it was an almost worldwide phenomenon. In the light of this increasing similarity to the first century it is not surprising that people should account for strange phenomena in themselves or in others as due to possession by a demon.

Belief in demon-possession has in some way continued right through the centuries from before the Christian era until our own day. There are many accounts of possession in the Middle Ages and later. One thing which turns up again and again is the infective nature both of the belief and of the phenomenon. Curiously convents were often the seat of supposed demon-possession. When one nun believed herself possessed, she seemed to infect others so that they believed the same. It is then likely that when so much attention is paid to demon-possession and exorcism by the media that one outbreak should lead to another, for the whole nation is a kind of closed community, and information about what happens in one part of the community is quickly spread by the media to other parts. We should then expect that demon-possession would be infective.

Finally we must enquire whether we are to disbelieve the stories in Scripture of demon-possession. In the light of what has been said there is no reason to do so. But that does not mean that we have to believe in the existence of demons themselves. The different books of the Bible were written within a culture in which certain views were held, and those views naturally coloured the truth of God as expressed by the writers. We accept this in many of the areas with which Scripture deals.

Few people, whether they wish for women ministers or not, would today rebuke a woman for taking part in a religious gathering; yet see 1 Timothy 2. 11, 12 and 1 Cor. 14.35. Silence on the part of women in society was altogether different then from what it is regularly accepted as authority and pattern for the sending out of missionaries today. We do not, however, insist that the pattern is literally followed. We allow them to take shoes, we give them money, we would think them foolish if they took only one shirt, though Mt. 10. 5-10 forbids all these. What was the recognised garb and behaviour of a holy man in Syria in the first century may not be effective in preaching the Gospel in the twentieth century in other parts of the world. Indeed, when this very passage appears in the Gospel of Mark and becomes a pattern to missionaries in Italy rather than Syria, they are told to take shoes. Genesis Chap. 1 says that the world was created in six literal days; few Christians believe this today, but they still accept the basic truth of the chapter that it was God, the God of Abraham, Isaac and Jacob, the God of the Exodus, who created the world. Demons were a part of the thought world of the first century; they belonged to the culture of the writers of Scripture. It was only natural that the writers should believe in them and repeat stories of the exorcisms carried out by Jesus and the disciples. The stories are still useful in those areas of the world where men believe in demons. They are assured by them that the power of Christ is stronger than any demon and that they can be freed from demonic influence.

But for most people who live in modern industrial society it must be recognised that the stories are irrelevant. It may sound wrong to say that Scripture can be irrelevant, but a moment's thought will show that this is not so. To most Christians in Western Europe the larger part of the Book of Revelation is irrelevant. They may read the letters written to the seven churches in Chapter 2 and 3, they may use some of the hymns of praise to Christ and God in the following chapters and they may be comforted at a funeral by the picture of the New Jerusalem in the closing chapters, but a great part of the imagery of the central chapters passes them by. Revelation was written for Christians who were being persecuted; we in Britain do not suffer persecution for our Christian faith. But wherever Christians have been persecuted they have found that many passages in Revelation which we pass by become relevant again to them. The description which Paul gives in 1 Cor. 11 of the way in which the Lord's Supper was celebrated in utter disorder is largely irrelevant to us. Paul talks of how those who came to the service divided themselves up into little groups which hardly talked to one another and of how some became drunk during the service. Nothing like that happens in our churches today. If there are abuses in our practice they are quite different. Some Christians approach the Bible thinking they have to accept everything which is in it, and make no allowance for cultural change, the change between the first century and our century. Because then they read of demons in Scripture they believe they ought to accept the existence of demons today and may go on to conclude that they or their friends are demon-possessed when in fact their 'sickness' may be explained in other ways. Were there not a past record of belief in demon possession it is doubtful if anyone in our Western industrial culture would today believe in such possession. We are conditioned by the past.

6

THE INTERPRETATION OF TONGUES

We do not possess a large amount of information about the worship of Christians in the early days of the church and most of what we do comes from First Corinthians. In it Paul answers various questions raised by the Corinthians, among them one about spiritual gifts. We ought probably to envisage a small group meeting in a house (cf. 1 Cor. 16.19; there would have been a number of such 'house-churches' in Corinth). In these meetings the Christians present made various contributions to the worship according to their abilities, or, more correctly, their spiritual gifts, *charismata*.

The Corinthians ask for Paul's guidance in their exercise. Probably he himself had introduced the concept of spiritual endowment to the Corinthians when he first brought the gospel and remained some time to build them up in the faith, for he has no hesitation in accepting the idea and it is found again in his letter to the Roman church (12.5ff.). In his answer to the Corinthians he attempts to clarify what these charismata are, to indicate their manifold nature and to show their relationship to one another. The Corinthians themselves have been concerned principally with the gift of speaking in tongues — glossolalia. In chapter 12 Paul begins by expounding the origin in God of these gifts (12.4-11) and points to their great variety (12.4-11, 28-30). They are to be exercised not only in the worship of the church but also in its administration and daily life ('helpers, administrators', 12.28), and those who exercise these charismata of whatever kind are to use them in such a way that the whole community is benefited (12.12-27). It is here that for the first time in his extant writings Paul introduces the concept of the church as the body of Christ. If the body is to be an organic and harmonious unity, then each gift is necessary and no gift has precedence over any other; so he emphasises that those gifts which appear to attract less attention should be honoured as much as those which everyone can see and admire. There is no gift which every Christian will possess by the simple fact that he is a Christian, nor can it be said that because a Christian does not exercise some particular gift, e.g. prophecy or tongues, that he is not therefore a Christian; nor is it to be expected that a true Christian will manifest them all.

At this point in 1 Corinthians we find the hymn to love; whether Paul wrote it at this time for this precise context, or wrote it earlier and takes it up now, or borrows it with or without adaptation from some earlier Christian does not matter to us. Love is not itself one of the charismata; it belongs to another, probably higher, category, though it resembles the charismata in being a gift of the Spirit. The hymn is used here to drive home the lesson that while different members of the community may have different gifts no gift can be exercised by a Christian without love, otherwise the church is injured and not aided. Unlike the charismata of which different ones are exercised by different believers, love is freely imparted to all (cf. Rom. 5.5) and should be displayed by all in their conduct towards one another, and of course towards the world outside the community.

Paul then goes on in chapter 14 to deal more directly with the gift of tongues; this he does by comparing its place in worship with the gift of prophecy. The latter is often taken to be the equivalent of modern-day preaching. This is an inadequate understanding. It is better to relate it to revelation: the prophet discloses God's will for man now and in relation to the future; the element of prediction cannot be excluded, and the prophets of the NT regularly predict future events.[1] Because of its revelatory nature the value of prophecy in building up the community is not in dispute between Paul and the Corinthians. Paul's criterion in estimating the relative importance of tongues and prophecy thus becomes their ability to 'build up' the community. Tongues do not achieve this purpose. Since they are addressed to God and not man (14.2, 6, 9) and are in a language which man cannot understand without an interpreter (14.27), they cannot benefit him. This might seem a totally adverse judgment but Paul's view is not so simple. Tongues are addressed to God and therefore they may help the speaker himself (14.4); Paul acknowledges that he himself has the gift (14.18), though he thinks it much better to speak five words that people will understand than to pour forth a torrent of tongues. Again, Paul lays down regulations for the use of tongues in worship, as he does for prophecy, and so acknowledges their value (14.27-32). He also apparently refers to them when in chapter 13 he speaks of the tongues of angels; probably the Corinthians have used this phrase to describe glossolalia and Paul picks it up as he often picks up the terms of others; it is not then clear whether he regards it as a correct description; the point of his argument is to drive home the necessity of love. Paul's own position is probably summed up best in the concluding words of the chapter: 'So, my brethren, earnestly desire to prophesy, and do not forbid speaking in tongues; but all things should be done decently and in order' (14.39, 40).

We have not yet identified what this gift of tongues actually is. That it cannot be understood by fellow-worshippers, that it is spoken apart from mental process (v. 14), that an interpreter is necessary if others are to understand — all this suggests that it corresponds to what we today know as speaking in tongues,

---

[1] cf. Best, 'Prophets and Preachers', *SJT* 12 (1959), 129ff.

a phenomenon which has appeared in all denominations and not merely in the so-called Pentecostal. At times, however, the glossolalia of 1 Cor. 14 has been taken to be the same as what appears to be intended in Acts 2 where the disciples are depicted as speaking in foreign languages. But if this is what it had been Paul would hardly then have criticised it since it would have been so useful in evangelism and certainly could not have been described as speech to God alone. (A great part of the importance of the gift of Pentecost in Acts 2 was its usefulness in the proclamation of the Gospel). It is proper to say here that in modern glossolalia there are two types, private and public; the latter since it occurs in worship requires interpretation; the former does not. The difficulty in understanding Paul may come partly from his failure to make this distinction clear.

To the listener the gift of tongues will have appeared strange; the speaker obviously uses sounds, the sounds appear to fall into some kind of grammatical structure, yet nothing can be understood. At times the speaker may appear to be in a trance, though this is by no means necessarily always true. To the speaker, and here the author depends for information at second-hand, there is something of importance in what he says, he believes he is talking sense, and through his experience he receives release of mind and soul and is filled with a deep sense of abiding joy.

So far so good, but what is to be said about all this? The report of a special committee of the United Presbyterian Church in the U.S.A. to their General Assembly of 1970 provides a carefully balanced conclusion:

> We therefore conclude, on the basis of Scripture, that the practice of glossolalia should be neither despised nor forbidden; on the other hand it should not be emphasised nor made normative for the Christian experience. Generally the experience should be private, and those who have experienced a genuine renewal of their faith in this way should be on their guard against divisiveness within the congregation. At the same

time those who have received no unusual experiences of the Holy Spirit
should be alert to the possibility of a deeper understanding of the gospel
and a fuller participation in the gifts of the Spirit — of which love is the
greatest.

Attention needs to be given to the opening words: 'We
therefore conclude, *on the basis of Scripture . . .*'. Underlying
this is the assumption that whatever can be shown to have been
a practice found in, and at any rate commended to some extent
by Scripture, cannot be dismissed. It is well known that there
are many Christians who look down on glossolalia, describe it
as gibberish proceeding from unbalanced and uncultured
minds and therefore consider it ought to be rejected by all
intelligent Christians. Clearly they have a different attitude to
Scripture. It may not be so well known but the Reformers, who
can hardly be regarded as not paying sufficient respect to
Scripture, also dismissed glossolalia.[1] This too is the verdict of
many conservative scholars today.[2] They regard it as a genuine
gift of the Spirit but one which was intended only for the
founding period of the church, i.e. they do not deny its
existence but regard it as so firmly placed in the first century
that we cannot expect to see it reproduced today; indeed some
of those who take this position regard the modern manifestations of glossolalia as induced by the devil.[3] These differing
conclusions on the place of glossolalia really depend on different theories of how Scripture is to be interpreted, i.e. they
employ different hermeneutical keys to unlock Scripture.

The title of this paper was deliberately intended to be
ambiguous. Paul mentions the interpretation of tongues and
argues for its necessity where tongues are used in public
worship, but there is another sense in which tongues have to

[1]See Calvin on Mark 16.17, which of course he took to be canonical. Calvin's statement
is somewhat qualified. Later Reformers were more absolute in their expressions.
[2]cf. M. F. Unger, *New Testament Teaching on Tongues* (Grand Rapids, Mich., 1972), pp.
23f.
[3]Unger, op. cit., pp. 1ff.

be interpreted: How are we to interpret glossolalia for our-selves? The point can be brought home with an illustration: strict conservatives who deny glossolalia as relevant to us today probably also argue that women should wear hats in church and should not be ministers; ardent advocates of glossolalia rarely deny to women the right to use this spiritual gift and probably are quite happy to see them in church whether they have hats on or not. How do we know which prescriptions in Scripture are to form the basis of our conduct? In what way are they to do so? There are in fact two related questions here: one asks after the authority of Scripture, and the other after its interpretation in the modern situation.

We do not intend to attack these questions directly but to come at them in a roundabout way. Whenever Protestant interpretation of Scripture has been carried out seriously it has been governed by two principles: (1) Scripture is its own interpreter; (2) the meaning of Scripture is the literal mean-ing.[1] Catholic interpretation has tended traditionally to add a third principle which in practice came to control the other two: interpretation must follow the line which the magisterium says is true. Tradition was therefore given a very high place. Despite their official rejection of such a principle Protestants have in fact allowed it to influence them, and so there has emerged in the course of exegetical history since the Reformation recog-nisable Lutheran, Reformed, Anglican, Baptist, Methodist traditions of interpretation. But we need not concern ourselves with these traditions but take up only the official principles of Protestant exegesis.

Quite clearly there has been a considerable change in the understanding of Scripture since the time of the Reformers, so if we work with these two principles we must allow for this change as we interpret. The development of the historical

[1] e.g., cf. R. M. Grant, *The Interpretation of the Bible* (London, 1965), pp. 102ff.

critical method from the nineteenth century onwards has made us see clearly what the Reformers only dimly glimpsed — the situational orientation of Scripture: all that is written in Scripture was directed to a precise historical situation and must be understood in the light of that historical context. This seems perfectly natural to all biblical scholars today though it is doubtful if its full consequences have yet been drawn for our understanding of the authority of Scripture and its interpretation. That it was not so obvious to the Reformers can be seen at once in the way in which in scholastic Protestantism Scripture came to be regarded as divine truth revealed in propositional form. Propositions have universal validity and therefore can be divorced not merely from their written context but also from their historical context — their situation — and applied to every situation. Hence, though wearing hats in church for women was originally anchored to a precise situation in Greece in the first century, it could easily become a proposition, and therefore applicable to every situation.

We take up first the principle of the plain meaning of Scripture. We can quickly dispose of certain false ideas. We must distinguish between poetic expression, parabolic expression and the plain meaning; such distinctions had already been drawn in the medieval period, worked out in response to the extremes of allegorical interpretation which had plagued exegesis from early days. Allegorical meaning was still accepted but only under certain restraints (e.g. it must be used only to confirm and not to establish doctrine). The literal meaning was always the primary meaning, and the literal meaning is the meaning intended by the author. If the author uses poetic imagery it is not to be taken literally because he did not intend it literally.

Now if we relate this literal meaning to the situational orientation of scripture the procedure of interpretation is not so straightforward as it might appear. When Paul ordered women in Corinth to keep their heads covered what was his intention? The interpretation of the passage in 1 Cor. 11 about women having their heads covered in church is very much disputed by scholars. Did Paul think only prostitutes went with uncovered head and was therefore zealous to preserve the good name of the church? Was Paul seeking to introduce the Jewish custom by which women were always veiled in public, and presumably he did this because he had been brought up to see this as God's way? Is it because in worship glory must be given only to God, and woman's hair, if it was seen, might distract man or the angels from this primary objective? Is it because the veil on her head represents her authority from God which allows her to take part in worship, and therefore again she wears it to fulfil God's will? When any of these interpretations is pushed we end by coming back to some primary intention: to do God's will, to further God's worship, to follow God's way. Within a concrete situation this primary intention is crystallised in a particular way — it is this crystallisation which is Scripture. What then was the intention of Paul? Surely it is the ultimate intention, an intention which can only be expressed in a very general way. What Scripture does is to provide examples of how this intention was worked out in a particular situation — and often to supply us with what, drawing on another context, may be termed 'middle axioms'. In Paul's description of worship the middle axiom would be the need for orderly worship. But worship can become over-orderly and lack spontaneity. This can never therefore be more than a middle axiom.

We have therefore now to ask about the Corinthian situation? Is it the same situation as ours? If so we can easily transfer Paul's instruction to our case. There are in a general kind of way situations which are the same then as they are now. If the situation is my position before God's justifying grace, then it is the same as a Christian in Corinth because we are both sinners — though our sins are very different in actual content. But there are few situations that are as general as that, especially when we ask the question: What ought we to do? A personal anecdote may illustrate this: I was crossing the sea of Galilee with some friends. One was eating toffees and throwing the papers overboard. I said to him, 'Would Jesus have done that?' He didn't really answer me but the reply could have been — 'Jesus never had any toffee papers!' The world has changed so much in twenty centuries that to take as a method of guidance, 'What would Jesus have done?', 'What would Paul have said?', simply will not work. There are other difficulties as we shall see later.

If Scripture is situationally oriented nothing, absolutely nothing, can forbid us asking after its situation. But how far can we go? We may say that these Christians in Corinth were young converts, that the church was not yet a stable community, that it was mostly composed of the poor and uneducated, that many of its members were slaves. But we need to be careful here for we cannot move from statements of that type to statements such as: 'For such a kind of people the emotional release which glossolalia brought was valuable': and then write tongues off. It is impossible to go back to first-century Corinth and examine individually the converts, but we can see what psychologists and sociologists have to say about glossolaliacs today, and, lacking any other information, assume that those in Corinth were psychologically similar. Some psychologists at any rate tell us that psychiatric tests do not show present-day glossolaliacs to be mentally unstable, but that in many cases they are the more mentally stable within congregations (though whether this was true of them before they became glossolalics or not cannot be determined, nor can it be shown that their stability comes from their being able to speak in tongues since there are present with tongues usually other gifts of the Spirit). The sociologists will tell us that glossolaliacs do not belong necessarily today only to the poorer classes: as a phenomenon glossolalia broke out first recently in the U.S.A. in Episcopalian and Presbyterian churches whose members have the highest 'wealth' rating. Nor do they belong to the uneducated; their main centres of activity in the U.S.A. are university campuses. Nor are they just young converts: many ministers of twenty and more years standing are glossolaliacs. Nor are they people lacking liturgical interest: the movement has spread widely in the Roman Catholic church. Nor are they necessarily fundamentalists, though there is, it appears, a tendency among them to accept Scripture as true (that would not have applied to the Corinthian converts because they did not possess Scripture with the same fullness we do). If then the individual make-up of the believer is a part of the situation and we cannot interview individual believers of Paul's time and have to infer what they were like from people who do similar things today, then certainly we cannot attribute glossolalia only to those with weaker characters, and in that way dismiss it.

But the total situation is not that of the character of the individual. There is the general cultural pattern of the time. Here we can only speak in broad terms: the old religious ways were disappearing; new religions, the mystery cults, were coming in from the east; gnostic ideas were beginning to manifest themselves. Corinth was a great centre of trade where this ferment had probably proceeded further than in many places. Society as a whole was probably unstable in its religion. Where religion existed it tended to centre on ritual and on experience rather than on morality. Ritual has obviously no bearing on our problem but experience has. Various forms of ecstasy were known in ancient religion; people were believed to be possessed; sometimes something very like glossolalia appeared;[1] prophecy was known; spiritual healing took place. It was therefore probable that something like these should appear in any new religion. This is not to say that glossolalia only appeared among the first converts in Corinth because they saw it in the world around them; it may have begun spontaneously with them independently of its appearance elsewhere. But because of the cultural situation in Corinth there was a strong likelihood that religion would be manifested in forms which we would term ecstatic or possessed. (We should note that in many religions untouched by Christianity such forms still appear.[2]) Presumably Christians then would have ascribed these phenomena outside Christianity to the work of evil spirits and disposed of them in that way (cf. 1 Cor. 12.3); it is more difficult for us to do so.

We turn now to the other principle of interpretation — Scripture is its own interpreter — that is to say that where we come on a difficult passage we look for easier passages within Scripture by which we may interpret it. No one doubts there are passages whose plain meaning is difficult to determine, and no one doubts that there are passages which are relatively easy to understand. While this is a principle which obviously applies to the interpretation of any author the Reformers saw it as having special reference to Scripture. To them Scripture was no ordinary book; its ultimate author was God. Therefore if a believer could not easily understand him at one place he might understand that place with the help of others where the same God was speaking. This clearly depends on a view of all Scripture as equally inspired by God. The principle, however, is not as straightforward as it appears to be. If we possess a writing in an unknown language, then we have to discover its meaning from an internal discussion of the writing itself. This

---

[1] cf. E. R. Dodds' essay, 'Supernormal Phenomena in Classical Antiquity', in his *The Ancient Concept of Progress and Other Essays* (Oxford, 1973), pp. 202f and the literature quoted there. See also *Theological Dictionary of the New Testament* ed. G. Kittel, trans. G. W. Bromiley. (Grand Rapids, Mich., 1964), vol. 1, pp. 722ff.

[2] cf. I. M. Lewis, *Ecstatic Religion* (London, 1971).

is how codes are broken; in this way also Minoan Linear B was deciphered (if it was deciphered). But the New Testament is not in that position. It is written in a language in which many other books have been written. We can therefore find out the meaning of most of the words in it from literature outside it — and Calvin was a good secular Greek scholar. The discovery of the Greek papyri at the end of last century led to the elucidation of some passages previously regarded as obscure. Thus the circle is not and cannot be complete. This is not to say that words like *charis* do not take on a special meaning within certain parts of the NT, but that as an absolute rule the principle that Scripture is its own interpreter is not rigid. An additional qualification is necessary. One of the advances of the historical-critical method has been the realisation that each of the writers of Scripture is an author in his own right; the way in which he uses a word or a concept may not be the same as the way in which another NT writer uses it.[1]

These criticisms of the principle do not mean we discard it; clearly those who wrote the NT wrote out of an experience which had common elements — the experience of Jesus as Lord — though they will have expressed this experience in different ways because of the differing situations in which and to which they wrote. On the other hand, the fact that the Reformers drew on the general knowledge of Greek in the Renaissance period to interpret the NT must itself be widened into the area of experience; in order to understand an experience or an idea in the NT we may have to look to see if light can be thrown on it by similar or parallel experiences or ideas in the ancient world as a whole, recognising also that just as *charis* has a special NT meaning so there may also be special

---

[1] One of the faults of a certain type of biblical scholarshipe is its failure to recognise this and therefore its easy paralleling of texts from different NT writings. This is another aspect of the situational view of Scripture; a writer's language is a part of his situation.

NT experiences and ideas. This would then bring us back to looking at experiences of ecstasy and possession in relation to healing, prophecy and tongues. We have already seen that these existed and we need not go back on this now.

If we applied the principle in its original sense we would probably move directly from the tongues of Corinth to the tongues of Pentecost. Do either throw light on each other? At the time of the Reformation Acts 2 was used to interpret 1 Cor. 14 — i.e. tongues was regarded as speaking in another existing language which could be understood by people. Because it was given this character it was regarded as appropriate only to the first days of the church. But few scholars today regard the underlying experience in Acts 2 as foreign language speaking, though they do not dispute that Luke understood it in that way. Today it is Acts 2 which is the difficult passage and 1 Cor. 14 is used to explain it. 1 Pet. 4.10 throws little light; 1 Thess. 5.19-21 implies the existence of charismata, in particular of prophecy, but does not allow us to draw any conclusion about tongues. But in Rom 12.5ff. Paul again refers to charismata and relates them to the image of the church. The list of charismata is different, but the fact that Paul writes to a church he had not visited about these charismata suggests that this subject appeared normally in his teaching and in that of other early Christian missionaries. Though prophecy is present in Rom. 12 tongues is missing. Thus writing to Rome where Paul knows less about the situation he does not mention the gift of tongues, and this accords with the relatively unimportant position he gives it in Corinth. He refers to them in Corinth because he knew that they had appeared in that city and is prepared to list them among the charismata, though he may not have taught about them on his original mission (probably they manifested themselves while he was present and he himself shared in the gift, hence his allusion in 1 Cor. 14.18 to speaking in tongues himself more than the Corinthians do).

Acts 2 does, however, allow us to infer that tongues were known in areas other than Corinth, probably at least in Jerusalem. We may fairly conclude that for Paul charismata were a necessary part of Christian experience, though an individual or a whole community could well exist without any particular charisma.

Our principles have brought us some distance on our way, but not all we need to go. We require to return now more directly to the situationally oriented nature of Scripture. Our situation is not the same as that of the Corinthians. It is unnecessary to drive this home. Anyone who has worked with biblical material knows that there are presuppositions in Scripture about the world of its time which no one would hold today; man himself is regarded in a different way. Apart from all that there is a formal difference: we know of their situation but they knew nothing of ours. What is written in the Bible about the Corinthians, or any other group, is itself a factor in our situation, and the more authority we give to it, the more powerful a factor is it in our situation. The existence of tongues in the early church is part of our situation.

Now we need to look at the remainder of our situation. We have already seen that the kind of people who speak in tongues in our situation are not exceptional in any way; we cannot conjecture any actual difference in their psychological make-up. We looked at the social situation then; what then about our own?

There is a certain superficial similarity in that now as then there is a rapidly changing religious situation in which traditional patterns are disappearing and in which strange sects, magic, astrology and witchcraft are beginning to flourish. We shall not dwell on this though it resembles the first century since situations are never really the same, but instead point out what appears to be one relevant factor in our total cultural situation. If we read Milton, we can follow his imagery because it is almost entirely drawn from the Bible or from classical Greece and Rome. A knowledge of this common cultural fount of imagery can no longer be depended on in readers nor is it used by writers. For their imagery the poets and artists of today more often draw from within themselves than from what in the normally accepted sense is common to all men. In a paper this can be more easily illustrated from literature than from art; it is also more relevant since in tongues we deal with words. We begin with a short quotation from Joyce's *Ulysses*:

What other infantile memories had he of her?

15 June 1889. A querulous newborn female infant crying to cause and lessen congestion. A child renamed Padney Socks she shook with shocks her moneybox: counted his three free moneypenny buttons one, tloo, tlee: a doll, a boy, a sailor she cast away: blond, born of two dark, she had blond ancestry, remote, a violation, Herr Hauptmann Hainau, Austrian army, proximate, a hallucination, lieutenant Mulvey, British navy.[1]

The connexions by which we move from one phrase to another are not those of normal rational speech which anyone can understand but depend on the inner consciousness of the character (Bloom is meditating on Millicent's mind). They are those of a stream of consciousness which is peculiar to one person.

It is necessary to introduce two technical terms. A *dialect* is a language in which people can communicate with one another; an *idiolect* is a language which is peculiar to one person, a language which in some cases he may deliberately invent.

'Twas brillig, and the slithy toves
    did gyre and gimble in the wabe:
All mimsy were the borogoves,
    and the mome raths outgrabe.

Everyone knows that this comes from *Alice Through the Looking Glass*. It sounds pleasant but it really has no meaning. It is an idiolect. The same kind of thing is found in Tolkien's

[1]Penguin edition, pp. 613f.

Lord of the Rings. Two lines are sufficient to demonstrate it:
> Annon edhellen, edro hi ammen!
> Fennas nogothrim, lasto beth lammen!
> (Part I, The Fellowship of the Ring, Bk. 2, Ch. 4)
> (cf. the long elvish song in Part I, Bk. 2, Ch. 8)

It would not be right to suggest that this is the same as glossolalia, but the books mentioned are all widely read and widely admired, the last two especially among young people. There are many other ways in which idiolects appear: the nonsense talk and rhymes of children; the meaningless syllables uttered by people who have lost their temper and who do not have a sufficient reserve of profanity to express themselves; the nonsensical words of refrains to many songs (and the lyrics of pop music).[1] The implication is that we should not be surprised to find idiolects appearing in religious contexts. Young people are used to them — and if we enjoy *Alice* let us not be too hard on glossolaliacs![2]

This means that we live in a situation today in which idiolects are likely to appear; this is a way in which people have begun to express themselves. And since this type of literature and art finds as ready an acceptance, if not a readier, among college and university students than anywhere else we should not be surprised to find glossolalia among the well-educated. When you add to this the hermeneutical principle accepted by most ordinary Christians that because it happened then it ought to happen now we can see that the ground for the appearance of glossolalia stands ready fertilised.

If it is not surprising that tongues should appear in our present culture and their exercise be found beneficial by many Christians, there is still the all-important question: Are they in

---

[1] See W. J. Samarin, *Tongues of Men and of Angels* (New York, N.Y., 1972).

[2] Since the first draft of this paper was compiled the writer has met a well-known NT scholar who has taught himself the technique of speaking in tongues. He can speak in several 'languages'; he regards this as a purely natural phenomenon and can exercise the technique at will.

our situation a good thing? Many people object to modern art and find it incomprehensible; some people are turned on by some modern art and left cold by large parts of it. Again it is not surprising that some Christians should find in tongues a way of expressing themselves in prayer and worship which brings them joy and release. That still does not answer the question as to its value, for drugs can bring release and joy to some people. There is, however, a more fundamental question than the one we have asked: Are tongues really a manifestation of the Spirit?

Here we must go back to almost the beginning of what has been said about exegesis. If the literal meaning of Scripture is the meaning intended by the author, it was presumably Paul's intention when he was writing about charismata to say that in the activities of Christians when they administered charity, when they governed the church, when they taught, prophesied, healed or spoke in tongues, they were not doing this wholly of themselves but that the Spirit was at work in them. Since he gives lists of charismata and these lists vary between Romans and 1 Corinthians we should not take either of them individually or both together as stating all the charismata that might exist, or as defining all those that ought to exist in every situation. (Some Neo-Pentecostalists refer to the 'nine' gifts of 1 Cor. 12.8-10; others do not make this restriction.) What Paul is doing is to list charismata appropriate to certain situations. Should we expect to see the same charismata today? If we look at his lists we see they relate to the internal life of the community except in so far as teaching, prophesying, healing may be regarded as also missionary activities directed outwards from the community. Today because of our situation we expect the church to be engaged in activities in the world which are less directly related to evangelism and we expect individual members of the church to take their place in the general activities of mankind, in politics, in industry, in the media, in the arts. Ought we not then to expect that there should be charismata in respect of these activities — the charisma of the trade unionist, the charisma of the politician, the charisma of the journalist? It is true that some of those who are leaders in these fields are said to have a 'charisma' — but that is not what Paul would have meant by the word.

An example will perhaps help. In certain circles in Ireland, both Protestant and Catholic, the neo-Pentecostalist movement has made considerable progress. Those who have been affected have been largely politically neutral, i.e. they have not adhered to violent policies; in their pulpits, if ministers, they have spoken of law and order; they have ministered to those who have suffered whether belonging to their side or not; they have prayed with one another across sectarian boundaries; yet they have not been active to seek a political solution. It would be wrong to say that their glossolaliac activities have been an escape from the real and terrible political problems which face Ireland and to the solution of which the church for years has failed to give adequate and clear guidance, but if Paul were to list the charismata necessary for the Church in Ireland today it is probable that right at the top of the list would come a political charisma. We cannot deny that there are some with this gift of God, but they are few and far between, and it is necessary also to say that there are those in the neo-Pentecostalist movement who would allow that such gifts should be desired by some Pentecostalists. It is in the light of this need for wider charismatic gifts and of the individual joy and heightened sense of God of glossolaliacs in Scotland that we must judge the usefulness of this particular gift here. No final judgment will be made in this paper.

At this point we can see that wider issues are involved, and the decision anyone makes on these will determine his decision on the present relevance of tongues to God's work. The first of these issues relates to the nature of charismata. Is a charisma a gift of the Spirit to a Christian which enables him to do something new which he could not do at all before? Or is it an inborn ability which is heightened because the man has become a Christian? The preacher will suffice as an example. It does not seem likely that on becoming a Christian his ability to put words together so as to prove persuasive should suddenly appear, but he would receive an insight into the gospel which he clearly did not previously possess and this coupled with his inborn persuasive ability, or ability gained through training in the use of words, would enable him to preach so that men would be converted and nurtured in the gospel. In the case of the charisma of administration the recipient does not suddenly attain an ability to administer but he attains a new way of doing it - in love. But it may not quite have appeared like that in Paul's day. Remembering the nature of those who became Christians, we can see that their recently gained ability to preach and administer seemed entirely new because they had never previously been in situations where their ability to speak or administer had been able to develop. In the Christian church they were now doing these things and this must have seemed a miracle. The gift of tongues also would not have been exercised by any of them in their pre-Christian days, and its sudden appearance would have seemed miraculous. Yet if we attribute some of the 'miracle' of the preacher and administrator to the Spirit must we not do the same for the glossolaliac? We can see what we attribute to the Spirit in the case of the administrator and preacher, but what in the case of the glossolaliac, especially if idiolects are not miraculous but natural? Tongues do not appear to be continuous with any previous ability.

A second wider issue must also be faced. Where does the Spirit operate? Only within the church (and this is the general answer of Scripture), or does the Spirit operate also outside the Christian community? Those who hold that the true sphere for the activity of the Spirit is the church will not exclude the prevenient activity of the Spirit in turning the hearts of sinners to God, but this is not what is at stake here. The question at issue is seen rather when we ask: Has the Spirit a share in the creative work of the artist? The church has never faced up to this question and those related to it; different Christians will offer varying answers.

But now we need to return to glossolalia. A number of options are open in the light of the views we take on the nature of charismata and the sphere of operation of the Spirit. We may decide that glossolalia is a natural phenomenon and not a charisma; it certainly brings joy and release from tension to some Christians, but to others the same will come through weeding the garden. We may decide that glossolalia is the activity of the Spirit whether it is found inside or outside the Christian community and so should be encouraged in both spheres. We may decide that glossolalia is a natural phenomenon outside the church but within the church there is an activity of the Spirit heightening the natural phenomenon. We may decide that it is a charisma within the church but where we find it outside then it is due to demonic influences. We may decide that Christian love is supernatural but glossolalia is natural. These are only a few of the options. It is important to realise that when we make our decisions we are bringing into play our theories, probably unconsciously held, on the nature of charisma and of the area of activity of the Spirit — in the end we bring into play our whole theology of the Spirit.

But this is not all that comes into play. Our reading of the sociological situation today will affect our view of tongues. Even more fundamentally there will be some who would argue that the sociological situation today has nothing to do with the matter and that in fact it is wrong to explore it.

If the argument of this paper has been followed up to now the reader will have realised that no answer to the question of the value of tongues is going to be provided. The purpose of the paper has not been to provide this but to do two other things: (i) to show the factors, often unconscious, which come into play when we try to make a decision about tongues; (ii) in a more general way to try and see how we unlock the Scriptures so that they speak to us today. How do we get from what Paul says about tongues to what the church should be saying today? Briefly what we have done is to look at a passage in Scripture and see how it is set in a particular situation; we have then tried to see what this has to do with us. Because of the situational nature of Scripture we have rejected a simple transference of what happened then to what ought to happen now. We have been forced to build up a picture of our situation. But our situation is not just a certain cultural situation; it is also a situation in which we already hold certain views about Scripture and its authority and about the Spirit and his activity in relation to the church and the world. When we attempt to move from Scripture to today we are inextricably involved in our own interpretation; there is no neutral way of making this movement. Even if we use as a key to unlock Scripture that what is advocated in it should always govern Christian thought and conduct, this itself involves the holding of a total theological position, and one which is not itself derived from Scripture but brought in from outside.

There is one further and very necessary qualification. To speak of each one making his own decision in the light of the total view he holds omits all reference to the church. Part of the frame of reference in which the individual Christian makes decisions about his own conduct and evaluates the conduct of others is the structure of the whole Christian community of which he is a member. To deny this would be to deny that Christian experience is corporate experience. The scholar may work at what Paul says, what the ancient world was like and what the world of today is like, yet the resolution of the problem cannot be left to him alone. The Reformation rejected rule by priests; rule by scholars would be a thousand times worse. What the scholar can do is to make us aware of the hidden presuppositions of our own cultural and ecclesiastical situation which come into play when we try to make up our minds, and of the more individual views that we have on theological, philosophical, aesthetic, political . . . matters and of which we are probably never aware (they may not even be consistent) but which determine the way in which our minds and wills work. This negative function is important and it is this which this paper has attempted to carry out.

7

THE COMMENTATORS AND THE GOSPELS

Our purpose herein is to do no more than examine how commentators actually handle the material in the Gospels and inquire after their objectives in commentating. For compactness and simplicity of examination we intend to restrict our survey to the Gospel of Mark. Four commentators have been chosen as representative: Matthew Henry,[1] V. Bartlet,[2] W. E. Bundy,[3] D. Nineham.[4] Henry wrote before the beginning of the modern critical movement; there is solid and detailed exegesis of the text, and though allegorisation is not absent yet it does not protrude unnecessarily. Whereas most commentators of the pre-critical period do not comment directly on the individual Synoptic Gospels, which is in itself significant and revealing, Henry does devote considerable space to Mark taken separately. It is a commentary which has had, and still does possess considerable influence in the pulpit; it would not be unfair to say that in their approach to exegesis the majority of preachers still resemble Henry more than any of the other representatives selected for examination. Bartlet fully accepts the priority of Mark, considering it to be based on the memories of Peter and thus to contain good historical material; while he does not believe it was written as a biography of

[1] *An Exposition of the Old and New Testament.*
[2] *St Mark*, Edinburgh, 1922.
[3] *Jesus and the First Three Gospels*, Cambridge, Mass., 1955.
[4] *Saint Mark*, London, 1963.

Jesus he quotes Burkitt with approval in his statement that it is 'an adequately historical outline of the main events' of the story of Jesus.[5] Both Bundy and Nineham write from the post-form-critical position which has accepted the argument of Wrede that the Gospel of Mark is primarily a theological document and that in it we encounter the faith of the early community: 'This tradition (of the Gospel material) reflects and records what was known and remembered, what was thought and felt, what was surmised and believed about Jesus by the early Christians a generation or more after his death'.[6] There is, however, as we shall see, a distinct difference of approach in these two commentators; Nineham is much more influenced by the Bultmannian rejection of the possibility of writing about the historical Jesus, and by the acceptance of Mark as an author in his own right.

We shall examine the account of the Baptism of Jesus as given by Mark (1.9-11):

9 And it came to pass in those days, that Jesus came from Nazareth of Galilee, and was baptized of John in Jordan.

10 And straightway coming up out of the water, he saw the heavens opened, and the Spirit like a dove descending upon him:

11 And there came a voice from heaven, saying, Thou art my beloved Son, in whom I am well pleased.

MATTHEW HENRY. His account is relatively brief, being about a quarter of the length he gives to the parallel story in Matthew. It was an underlying assumption of commentaries of this period that all the evangelists express the same point of view, that of the Holy Spirit. No individuality was accorded to them. Once Matthew had been dealt with in detail Mark did not need the same treatment.

Henry carefully takes each clause of the account separately and comments on it. His comments turn the words of Scrip-

---

[5] p. 66.
[6] Bundy, *op. cit.*, p. 579; cf. Nineham, *op. cit.* pp. 48 ff.

ture to his readers with moralising and theological applica-
tions.

> His *baptism*, which was his first public appearance, after he had long
> lived obscurely in *Nazareth*. O how much hidden worth is there, which
> in this world is either lost in the dust of contempt and cannot be known,
> or wrapped up in the veil of humility and will not be known! But sooner
> or later it shall be known, as Christ's was.

> He *saw the Spirit, like a dove, descending upon him.* Note, then we
> may see heaven opened to us, when we perceive the Spirit *descending* and
> working upon us. God's good work in us is the surest evidence of his
> good will towards us, and his preparations for us.

He pays no special attention to the words of the Heavenly
Voice. They are not to be considered more important than any
of the other words of the passage, for in reality all the words of
Scripture are words of the Heavenly Voice. In the Matthean
parallel he says a little about the words but assumes that 'Son'
means what it meant in the later creeds and takes it as a
testimony to the eternal generation of the Christ. He does not
discuss what it may have meant to Jesus. Henry accepts the
event as a whole and never defends its historicity; nor does he
apologise for it; even when he considers John's hesitancy to
baptize Jesus as portrayed by Matthew he seems to feel no need
to apologise for the event nor to indicate that the early church
may have been embarrassed by it.

BARTLET. Here we move in an entirely different atmosphere.
At the beginning of his comment the event is firmly set on the
plane of history by a discussion of the geographical identifica-
tion of Nazareth and of the probable spot on the Jordan where
Jesus would have been baptized. Most of the comment,
however, is devoted to setting the event into the life of Jesus
himself.

> As Jesus ascended from the stream which had, as it were, engulfed
> in his person the old past order or world in Israel's life — carried upon
> his soul, in vicarious sympathy, into the waters of repentance and re-
> consecration — God himself did there and then intervene with sensible
> tokens (to him) that the separation between earth and heaven was at

length annulled, and communion between them established such as was to mark the Messianic Age. For to Jesus' rapt gaze, as his eyes sought the heavens in silent prayer (Lk. 3.21) of adoration and trust in his heavenly Father, those heavens parted asunder and a dove-like form glided down towards himself, the token of Peace and Goodwill for men, as it had been to Noah in the former days, when a new earth rose out of the waters that had purged away the old order (cf. I Pet. 3.20ff for the general idea). Such was the vision which greeted his fresh self-dedication to his Father's will and its reign 'on earth as it is in heaven'; and following on it, a Voice, also coming as it seemed, from the heavenly regions, had testified at this moment of spiritual crisis to his own Sonship and the heavenly Father's perfect complacency in him. Such an experience must needs evoke a very tumult of feelings and thoughts, overwhelming in their strength, and needing time for reflection in order to yield up their true meaning, according to his Father's purpose. For it meant a new sense of special filial relation, probably also of Messianic vocation, which he now knew, perhaps for the first time with any assurance, to be involved in it.

The historicity of the baptism of Jesus is defended through an argument for its vicarious nature (alluded to in the above quotation) and by a reference to Is. 6.5 related to Jesus' 'sense of solidarity with God's people'. Mark's account is preferred to those of the other Gospels in which the experience is more objectified; Mark gives the 'first and simplest presentation'. Yet the other Gospels do give additional helpful information which is used (as in the reference to Lk. 3.2 above) since Bartlet is making an attempt through Mark's Gospel to reach what happened in the life of Jesus himself. There is thus: (i) An attempt to defend the historicity of the event; (ii) A search for its original nature; (iii) An explanation of what it must have meant for Jesus himself as his life developed. (iv) No lessons are drawn from the event to help his readers in their lives nor is the dogmatic significance of the event discussed.

BUNDY. Like Bartlet, Bundy uses the gospels to seek after the historical Jesus, but because he comes after the development of form-criticism he takes a much more sceptical attitude to the material in the gospels. Thus he distinguishes two stages in Mk. 1.9-11.

Mk. 1.9 is the original and primary tradition on Jesus' baptism . . .
Mk. 1.10-11 is a piece of secondary tradition . . . (it) confronts the reader
with the thought and theory of the early Christian church. It is simply
a piece of religious fiction which has no historical value except for the
nature of the religious faith from which it came and which found
expression in it. . . . It is a sort of aside which, at the beginning, lets the
reader in on the secret of the hero's true nature and identity: he is the Son
of God. . . . Verses 10-11 are simply the colourful first act in the
dramatised version of the Christian dogma of Jesus as the Son of God.

(Mk. 1.9) is a simple, sober statement of fact without qualification
or apology. There is no reason to doubt that Jesus was baptized by John.
That it is not an invention of the Christian imagination is clear in the
fact that later tradition was embarrassed by it (Matthew and Luke) or
suppressed it entirely (John). Mk. 1.9 is about as realistic and undogmatic
a notice as one could hope to find in a document devoted to the interests
of Christian propaganda.

Bundy clearly allows that Mark is dominated by a dogmatic
purpose but he is not interested in this; he is seeking to
disentangle the historical facts from the theological superstruc-
ture. He explains the meaning and purpose of the secondary
additions to the original tradition but quite obviously prefers
to consider the latter than the former. Because I.10-11 are a
later addition Bundy is unable to discuss the baptism as an
experience in the life of Jesus; he simply has no material on
which to work. He is at one with Bartlet in drawing no moral
or theological lessons for his readers, though he does envisage
Mark as intending many such lessons to be drawn by his
readers.

NINEHAM. The interests of Nineham are again different.
There is no comment on v. 9 and no discussion whether Jesus
was likely to have been baptised by John or not; the embarrassment of the other evangelists as noted by Bundy is not
mentioned nor is there any attempt to explain why Jesus might
have come to John to be baptized such as we found in Bartlet.

Just as St Mark showed no interest in John the Baptist except as the
forerunner of the Messiah, in vv. 9-11 he shows no interest in the events
he is describing except as proving the truth he wants to convey. He

makes no attempt, for example, to say what effect these events had on Jesus himself; did they, for example, constitute a 'call' or a sudden revelation about himself, or only a confirmation of views he had already formed about himself? On the basis of St Mark's account it is impossible to be sure and even idle to speculate.

There is a fuller discussion of vv. 10, 11:

> *The significance St Mark saw* (italics mine) in the fact was probably as explaining how Jesus could have been proclaimed Son by God himself and yet not recognised as such by men during the subsequent ministry; it is part of his theory of the 'messianic secret'.

The italicised words, and there are many similar phrases, give the clue to the use Nineham makes of the gospel material: he is intent to draw out what it meant for Mark and the community in which and for which he wrote. Thus he discusses what the words of the Heavenly Voice might have meant for a Christian of the first century, not what they may have meant to Jesus nor to the later faith of the church as formulated in its creeds and confessions. The words are set in the context of Mark and the primitive community and interpreted therefrom.

It we look back the way we have come we see that Nineham and Henry are at one in taking little or no interest in what happened in the original event; Bartlet and Bundy are agreed in seeking this, though they come up with very different results. Nineham and Henry, however, have completely different attitudes to the Heavenly Voice. Bartlet is alone in seeking to explain the baptism in terms of Jesus' own experience; Henry ignores this aspect; Bundy and Nineham consider the material for such an understanding simply does not exist. Nineham's primary aim is to set the incident in the context of the Gospel as a whole and interpret it from that angle; Bundy does this in part; both admit that Mark is governed by a dogmatic purpose but Bundy does not really like it, while Nineham seeks to draw it out and this process is for him the object of his commentary. Bundy, Nineham, and Bartlet comment at varying length on different parts of the pericope;

Henry comments on every detail with equal emphasis. Henry has no interest in the editorial work of Mark, either to comment on it or to eliminate it and so seek the historical Jesus more accurately.

How have these differing emphases arisen? We may note first the changing face of New Testament scholarship from Henry to Nineham. Between Henry and Bartlet lay the solution of the Synoptic problem and the two-document hypothesis; Mark is the earliest Gospel and as such must contain the most reliable information about Jesus; since its outline of the course of his ministry was accepted by Matthew and Luke it should be recognised as a faithful record; with it a life of Jesus can be written. Thus at this stage the gospels are used as material to seek the historical Jesus. Between Bartlet and Bundy, Wrede and the form-critics destroyed confidence in the Markan outline of Jesus' ministry; the incidents in the life of Jesus had circulated in the primitive church as individual pericopae and in this period they had lost those notes of time and place which were necessary if they were to be set again in a geographical and chronological order; the various form-critics found differing amounts of the material as reflecting Jesus himself, but all of it had been profoundly modified, if not created, by the primitive community; thus it told us much more about the primitive community than about Jesus. At best all we had was a number of pearls fallen from the connecting string which was lost for ever; we might have glimpses of the historical Jesus but no insight into the nature of his life and ministry; we could not explore his self-consciousness, simply because we did not have the material. Between Bundy and Nineham Redaktionsgeschichte became an established tool of scholarship. The individual pericopae might give access to the faith of the primitive community; the way in which Mark, who himself had no outline of the life of Jesus, put them together, allowed us to see what were his own particular interests and those of the community in and for which he composed his Gospel. Much work is now being done by scholars on all three Synoptic gospels from this angle.[7]

Such a description of the change in scholarship is not itself an explanation of the change. In part the explanation lies within the scholarship itself but even more it lies in the world of theology and the philosophy of history. Biblical scholarship, though at times it may claim to be neutral, has been much influenced by changing fashions in theology and philosophy. At these it is only possible to glance briefly.

The nineteenth-century belief in objective history — history as it really happened — was one of the factors in producing the search for the historical Jesus. When this became the chief pursuit of New Testament scholars and when each thought it was the crowning achievement of his life to produce a life of Jesus, then the gospels, as the most important source, became quarries for facts about Jesus and for the interpretation which he put on his own existence. Thus in the commentary of Bartlet, and the many others which resemble it, chief attention is given to what can be learned about the historical Jesus; Bartlet was reasonably conservative in his approach; other commentators took up a more radical attitude; in one sense, though much later, Bundy represents this radical attitude; he knows it is impossible to write a life of Jesus but he still believes that certain facts can be dug out from the gospels and it is part of his duty as a commentator to bring them to light.

The nineteenth-century belief in objective history did not last long into the twentieth century before undergoing severe attack. Not only was the lack of objectivity on the part of the historian recognized — for he brought his own world view

[7]E.g., G. Bornkamm, K. Barth and H. J. Held, *Tradition and Interpretation in Matthew*, P. Bonnard, *Évangile selon Saint Matthieu*, W. Marxsen, *Der Evangelist Markus*, H. Conzelmann, *The Theology of St Luke*.

through which he interpreted the facts before him — but the lack of objectivity in the historical sources had also to be allowed for. A birth certificate may be an objective fact but it is only important as the certificate relating to some person, and as soon as his thoughts and actions are set down the world view of the recorder enters. In particular this led to the recognition that the stories of Jesus as we have them are written from the other side of the resurrection; those who wrote about the earthly Jesus knew him also as the exalted Lord and this could not but affect their account; what passed almost unnoticed at the time would later take on an entirely new significance. With this came the realisation, and Martin Kähler had much to do with this, that the evangelists were not attempting to give lives of Jesus but to bring men to faith in Christ. If they were not attempting to write such lives was it a valid use of the material they provided to write such a life in the twentieth century? Combined with this was the result of the more radical critics that research into the forms of the Gospel incidents left little that was sufficiently sure or certain to be used in the reconstruction of a life of Jesus. If the material was not there and if the whole purpose of the search for the historical Jesus was suspect, it was only natural that a new use should be made of the Gospel material. So it was used firstly to record the faith of the early church[8] and then with the methods of Redaktionsgeschichte, to seek the faith of the evangelist himself. Since the gospels are written from faith to faith all we can learn from them is the faith of the first Christians, evangelist and community. Thus we have seen Bundy attributing a large portion of Mark's baptismal narrative to the early church and asking what the community took it to mean, and Nineham going further and seeking to interpret the gospel only for what we can learn of the faith of Mark and of the first Christians.

[8]Cf. Rawlinson's commentary on Mark.

But this is by no means the whole picture. To see it we need to return to Henry. For him the gospels were the word of God, a set of propositions which had to be interpreted for the benefit of his readers. He has no interest in history in itself, though he would certainly have affirmed that what is recorded in the gospels actually happened in the way it is recorded. Revelation lay before him in the words of the Bible. The critical work of the nineteenth century shattered any belief in a simple relationship between the words of Scripture and revelation. Revelation, instead, was held to lie in the actions which are recorded in Scripture. Scripture reports the acts of God and Scripture must therefore be used to discover the historical facts in which those acts took place. From this angle the search for the historical Jesus became a theological necessity, for here, as it were, God's action was most highly concentrated. Thus many commentaries, like Bartlet's were written to reach the central point of God's revelation — his dealings with men in Christ Jesus. Where all thought of revelation was abandoned Jesus was still recognised as a great man and much could be learned from his example; again this led to the search for what he actually said and did.

To this last emphasis in the liberal theology of the earlier part of the twentieth century came a reaction with Barth. His own work drew heavily on Scripture and he has produced many penetrating insights into its meaning. More importantly he argued for a close relationship between Scripture and the Word of God; the latter he saw under the threefold aspect of eternal Logos, written Word, and preached Word. Inevitably this produced a new emphasis on the exegesis of Scripture rather than on the search for the historical facts which lay behind it. Scripture is studied for its witness to the Word of God rather than for its witness to the life of Jesus, though by the very nature of the fact that the Word was made flesh as Jesus the two cannot be separated. This emerges clearly in Barth's hermeneutic where a Biblical hermeneutic is primary and from it a general hermeneutic is to be derived. Thus it is the exegesis of Scripture which is all important. At times this has seemed like a return to fundamentalism and Biblical scholars have often shuddered at what Barthian exegetes have done to texts. But Barth himself never intended such a result and his own exegesis has generally been superior to that of his disciples. This emphasis on the Word of God is then another factor in the climate which has turned attention to the words of the Gospels rather than to the events they record.

It must be confessed, however, that it has had less influence on New Testament scholarship than the existentialist approach of Bultmann. At an early stage Bultmann stood near to Barth but diverged gradually from him, as he came more and more to accept Heidegger's form of existentialism. True faith lies in self-understanding, and a man is brought to this by the cross of Jesus. Despite criticism from the more radical wing of Christian existentialism Bultmann has insisted that the fact of the death of Jesus cannot be eliminated; on the other hand he has refused to demand more than the 'that' of Jesus' death. In this attitude he can be seen to be supported by the view emanating from Kähler that the gospels are only passion narratives with introductions, and by his own New Testament work which left so little of the historical Jesus in the gospel reports. (It is interesting that in his insistence on the 'that' of the cross he is near to a certain brand of traditional theology which sees the death of Jesus as all-determinative in Christian faith, for which the blood of the cross is crucial and the teaching relatively unimportant; the difference — and it is a most important one — between this and Bultmann lies in the attitude taken to the resurrection.) If the 'that' of the cross is central and if the gospels are in effect the self-understanding of men faced with this fact, then they are studied not for the details they give about Jesus but for the self-understanding they have produced and are still producing. Thus it can be seen that Redaktionsgeschichte emerged logically from the Bultmann school. But it would be wrong to consider it a prerogative of that school alone. There is also much in the Barthian school which is sympathetic to the view that the evangelists are theologians rather than historians.

It would appear then that the signs indicate the emergence of commentaries which concentrate their attention on the editorial work of the evangelists. This does not mean that other commentaries will disappear. Even during the dominance of the historical commentary of Bartlet's type commentaries of the type of Matthew Henry continued to appear, and reprints of Henry himself and other puritan scholars still regularly appear in some publishers' lists. So we may expect that the historical commentaries will still be written. Moreover, the post-Bultmannian school with its new search for the historical Jesus is bound to turn back the attention of commentators to the words and actions of Jesus. The work will never be done as easily as Bartlet did it; today we realise how much more of the early church is in the gospels, whether it penetrated during the oral period or entered through the work of the evangelists themselves. This cannot be lightheartedly eliminated. Even if it could be, Bultmann still raises the question whether it ought to be; is not the 'that' of the cross sufficient? And here we return to the problem of faith and history. Bultmann's own position seems to be untenable.[9] On the one side there are those who go farther than he has gone and are prepared to eliminate the 'that' and to rest content with the faith of the early church; Jesus has no other existence than in the preaching. On the other side are the post-Bultmannians who find themselves compelled to resume the search for the historical Jesus because a 'that' which

[9]Bultmann has to some extent modified his original position.

is not attached to someone ends by not being even a 'that'; and if there is a 'someone' then his existence demands that we know something about him.

The future for those who wish to write commentaries on the gospels will not be easy, and very different commentaries will emerge from those who take opposed views on the relationship of history and revelation.

8

FASHIONS IN EXEGESIS: EPHESIANS 1:3

This is not an attempt either to present an exegesis of Eph. 1:3 or to trace the history of its exegesis. It is rather an attempt to see what particular issues occupied the attention of exegetes at particular times and if possible to account for some of these preoccupations. In order to carry this through and at the same time to limit the material I shall consider only the commentators and leave aside the more specialised material in monographs and articles in learned journals. New ideas tend first to appear in the latter and then work their way into commentaries, though it can often take quite an appreciable time for this to take place.Limitations of space forbid reference to every commentator. Many simply repeat what their predecessors have written with only minor linguistic variation. I shall therefore treat only those commentators who display new trends or stress old ones in a new way.

In English, Eph. 1:3 runs as follows:

> Blessed is the God and Father of our Lord Jesus Christ who has blessed us with every (all) spiritual blessing in the heavenlies in Christ.

It is only the beginning of a long sentence which runs through to verse 14. This raises the question of the relation of v. 3 to what follows. Within the verse itself there are certain issues which must be discussed. There is no copula ('is') in the original; what should be inserted? What is the significance of the 'and' between 'God' and 'Father'? Why do we have a past tense in 'has blessed' (which translates the Greek aorist participle)? To whom does 'us' refer? Is 'every (all)' inclusive? What is a 'spiritual' blessing? What are 'the heavenlies'? What noun should be understood with this adjective? Is 'in Christ' to be taken locally, corporately, mystically, instrumentally? Other problems will appear as we proceed. The manner in which I have set out at least some of these questions follows the methods of modern scholarship. That in itself is an instance of 'fashion in exegesis'.

The first known commentator on Ephesians is Origen. Only fragments of his commentary survive.[1] Fortunately a reasonably long discussion of our verse is extant, though we cannot be sure we still possess all that Origen wrote.

He says that some have taken the reference to spiritual blessings as an attempt to distinguish Christian blessings from those of Leviticus and Deuteronomy which are physical. He accuses the 'heterodox' of doing this but does not identify them more exactly. Since he goes on to indicate that this permitted them to separate God from such a view (i.e. God is not interested in the blessings of Leviticus and Deuteronomy) it is probable that he has in mind those who reject the Old Testament, the Marcionites. This is confirmed when he argues that even under the Law there were spiritual blessings quoting Rom. 7:14 and points out that the prophets did not obtain material blessings such as those instanced in Deut. 28 (their barns were not filled). He also used Heb. 11:37-38 to prove his point.

He then discusses 'the heavenlies' and quotes Phil. 3:20 with its reference to citizenship in heaven and Matt. 6:19-21 about those who lay up treasures in heaven. These texts are used repeatedly by the Fathers in discussing this phrase. Origen points out that we have a past tense in 'has blessed' and not the

---

[1]For an edited text see J. A. F. Gregg, 'The Commentary of Origen upon the Epistle to the Ephesians', *JTS* (old series) 3 (1902) 233-44, 398-420, 554-76.

future we would expect. He therefore suggests that 'in the heavenlies' should be understood as 'what is perceptible to the mind and beyond the senses'. He concludes that it is for our easier understanding of the passage that there is reference both to 'spiritual' and 'the heavenlies'.

A large part of the comment of Origen has been dictated to him by an existing controversy, the Marcionite view of God and of the Old Testament, and therefore emerges at least in part from the situation of the church of his time. This is a clear example of what this paper hopes to disclose in exegesis. We note also that finding difficulty with the second clause, particularly with the past tense of the participle, he translates it into a meaning which he believes people can understand. Whereas the reference to Marcion disappears from later commentaries the attempt to find a suitable understanding of the second clause does not.

Jerome[2] knew Origen's commentary, acknowledges his debt to it[3] and in many instances simply rewrites it. It is possible that where he appears to add material to what our fragments of Origen tell us he is simply repeating portions of Origen which no longer survive. The additions which concern our text seem to be accounted for more easily in other ways. He drops the reference to the 'heterodox'; they no longer bothered him or the church of his period. Like Origen he recognises that the Old Testament prophets did not enjoy material blessings and that therefore the blessings of that Testament cannot be restricted to those which are physical. In his discussion of the heavenly blessings he introduces several more passages from the New Testament, viz. John 15:19; 1 Cor. 15:49; Rom. 8:9. He draws attention to one element of importance over and above the discussion of Origen. God is both the God and

---

[2] *In Epistolam ad Ephesios* (*MPL* 26.467-590).
[3] Cf. Gregg, loc. cit., p. 233.

Father of our Lord Jesus Christ, i.e. the genitive is attached both to God and to Father. He was not necessarily the first to introduce this issue for we encounter it in other contemporary commentators. It arises almost certainly from the christological controversies of the period. If Christ is God can God be said to be his God? Jerome answers (others offer different answers) that God is God of the manward side of Christ and Father of the one who was Word of God from the beginning with God. Interestingly Jerome offers no grammatical arguments to sustain his view that the genitive is attached to both nouns. Long after the christological controversy has died down we find scholars in the modern period discussing this point in great detail but on grammatical grounds. There is then in Jerome and contemporary commentators an awareness of an exegetical problem, an awareness caused by contemporary theological concerns. It is not however possible to make a direct correlation of christological and grammatical views. Within the school of Antioch Theodore of Mopsuestia[4] and Theodoret of Cyrus[5] opt for the splitting of the reference to both God and Father and take the reference to God to be a reference to God as our God and that to Father to be one to him as Father of Christ; Chrysostom[6] however takes the phrase as one with God as God of the incarnate Jesus and Father of God the Word.

Theodore is interesting in other respects. He regards v. 3 as a thanksgiving like the generally recognised thanksgivings of Phil. 1:2; Col. 1:3; 1 Thess. 1:3; 2 Thess. 1:3. He does not comment on the renewal (?) of the thanksgiving at 1:15-16. We shall see discussion of this emerging much later. Theodore

---

[4] See H. B. Swete, *Theodore of Mopsuestia on the Minor Epistles of S. Paul*, vol. 1 (Cambridge, 1880), pp. 112-96.

[5] *Interpretatio Epistolae ad Ephesios* (*MPG* 82.505-57).

[6] *Ad Ephesios* in *Interpretatio Omnium Epistolarum Paulinarum*, vol. 4 (Oxford, 1852) pp. 104-365 (*MPG* 62.9-176).

explains 'blessed' as meaning that God is worthy to be praised. That he gives an explanation is curious for this is the normal meaning of the Greek root. What is not normal is its later use in the verse to indicate gifts by God.[7] The latter is a meaning derived from the Septuagint. Theodore joins together the two halves of the verse: God is worthy to be blessed because he has blessed us. This point which he is apparently the first to make recurs in many later commentators. He also discusses 'in Christ' and gives it an instrumental sense. More importantly he discusses the spiritual gifts in the heavenlies and isolates them as resurrection, immortality, the capability of not sinning, and the continual possession of good gifts. He thus places them in the future, concluding this from the reference to the heavenlies. But at this point he also brings in v. 4 in order to indicate something of the way God has blessed us. He thus begins a trend which identifies the blessings with blessings mentioned in vv. 3-14. By means of 1 Cor. 15:42-44 he relates 'spiritual' to the spiritual body which we have in the heavens. With him the possible difference between the blessings of the two testaments disappears, though this is by no means true of other Fathers. Chrysostom, for instance, denies that the Jewish blessings were spiritual and identifies the spiritual blessings as those of freedom, immortality, adoption, etc., picking up some of the themes of the succeeding verses. John 16:33 excludes any carnal blessings from their number. Without discussion Chrysostom and Theodoret do not give 'heavenlies' a local significance but refer to gifts, i.e. the noun to go with 'heavenlies' a local significance but refer to gifts, i.e. the noun to go with 'heavenlies' is not τόποι but πράγματα. Chrysostom now completely free from having to deal with

---

[7]Note the almost total absence of this meaning in classical lexica. See also H. W. Beyer, *Theologisches Wörterbuch zum Neuen Trestament*, vol. 2 (Stuttgart, 1935) p. 752; W. Schenk, *Der Segen im Neuen Testament* (Berlin, 1967) pp. 36 ff.

Marcionites contrasts the blessings of v. 3 with those of the
Jews and employs Heb. 3:5-6 to prove their superiority since
Christ is superior to Moses. He also introduces a new identi-
fication of the blessings which he deduces from other parts of
scripture as Christ's presence (John 14:23), as being built on
the rock (Matt. 7:24-25) and as being confessed before God by
Christ (Matt 10:32-33). In addition he draws in the beatitudes
(Matt. 5:3ff.).

There is another strain in the Fathers which concentrates on
exhortation rather than on exegesis and seems to have little to
do with theological controversy. This stream is first found in
Marius Victorinus Afer.[8] He moves from the phrase 'the
Father of our Lord Jesus Christ' to the sonship of Christians.
The reference to spiritual blessings in the heavenlies is used to
remove any idea that believers are necessarily blessed in this
world; Peter and Paul were not. Spiritual blessings belong to
the future. Although the persecution of Peter and Paul is
introduced there is no suggestion that spiritual blessings are
regarded as compensation for the sufferings of persecution.
With the exception of Origen all the other Fathers write from
a period when persecution was no longer a threat. Marius in
fact lies nearer the persecution period than any of them, except
Origen, and perhaps his introduction of Peter and Paul is the
reflection of an earlier exegesis, no longer extant, in which
spiritual blessings in heaven were contrasted with persecution.

We must now move on more quickly looking only at a few
commentators until we reach the modern period. Thomas
Aquinas[9] notes the difficulty presented by the past tense 'has
blessed' and explains it as Paul's certainty that God will bless
in the future. He gives no justification for such a use of the

---

[8] *In Epistolam Pauli ad Ephesios* (MPL 8.1235-94).
[9] *Opera omnia* ed. S. E. Fretté and P. Maré, vol. 21 (Paris, 1876) pp.260-343. ET by
Matthew L. Lamb (Albany, N.Y. 1966).

aorist. He shows no awareness of the frequent distinction in the Fathers between Jewish and Christian blessings and indeed uses Ps. 127:4 in his description of the blessings. His explanation of them is worked out in terms of efficient, material and final causes and so is governed by his general philosophical approach and terminology, an interpretation into the language of his own period and its type of understanding. Finally we should note that he is aware of the theological issue which lies in the 'and' of 'God and Father' and explains it.

While commentators of the Middle Ages are usually aware of what the Fathers have written Calvin[10] is the first of those we are examining who explicitly refers to them by name when he says he does not object to Chrysostom's contrast between the blessings of Moses and those of Christ. He notes that the adjective 'heavenlies' could be followed either by a word denoting place or gift and refuses to rule firmly in favour of one or the other. He includes a brief word study of 'bless' noting that it is used in four different ways in scripture: of men blessing God, of God blessing men, of men blessing one another in prayer, and of priestly blessings. He is aware that words can carry more than one meaning and that the context must determine between meanings. There is no theological discussion of 'God and Father'. This is true also of the commentary of H. Zanchius.[11] It is more surprising in his case since he did not restrict himself in any way as regards space. His is the longest commentary (some 750 pages) until Markus Barth. It is also surprising since he follows each portion of his exegesis with a set of theoretical conclusions (*loci theologici*). This has no section on Christology but a long one on soteriology,

---

[10] *Corpus Reformatorum* 79 (1895) *Calvini opera* vol. 51, pp. 141-240; ET by T. H. L. Parker, *The Epistles of Paul to the Galatians, Ephesians, Philippians and Colossians* (Edinburgh, 1965) pp. 121-224.

[11] *Commentarius in Epistolam Sancti Pauli ad Ephesios* (ed. A. H. de Hartog, Amsterdam, 1888; 1st ed. 1594).

presumably because while Protestants and Catholics agreed on the former they did not on the latter. So far as I am aware he is the first who points out that 2 Cor. 1:3 begins in the same way as Eph. 1:3 and that similar phrases commencing with 'blessed is' are to be found in the Old Testament and that we find this form in the New Testament in Luke 1:68.

J. A. Bengel[12] (1687-1752), as we might expect, begins to notice new aspects and wastes no words in his comments. The double use of 'bless' is an *antanaclasis*, a term which commentators have used ever since to display their learning! He notes the similarity of Eph. 1:3 with 1 Pet. 1:3 and points out that 1 Peter was also sent to Ephesus. He views vv. 3-14 as a summary of the epistle, a view which re-emerges in the twentieth century as if something new. He notes the recurrence of the word 'heavenlies' at other points in the letter but does not expand on this; he takes it to denote the glorious abode of the heavenly ones. He makes an explicit mention of a Trinitarian reference in the verse, the Holy Spirit entering through 'spiritual'.

G. C. A. Harless[13] may not have been the first genuinely modern commentator but he stands very near the beginning of the line. Since he treats the passage in great detail it is important to indicate the points he raises though not necessarily the conclusions he reaches. Of his commentary Charles Hodge[14] wrote 'This is the most elaborate commentary on this epistle which has yet been published. It is orthodox and devout, but is wearisome from its diffuseness and lack of force' (Hodge was fortunate that he did not have to read some of

---

[12] *Gnomon Novi Testamenti* (editio tertia recusa adjuvante Johanne Steudel, Tübingen, 1850).

[13] G. C. A. Harless, *Commentar über den Brief an die Epheser* (Erlangen, 1834).

[14] Charles Hodge, *A Commentary on the Epistle to the Ephesians* (Grand Rapids, 1980; 1st ed. 1856).

Harless's successors!). With Harless there is an entirely differ-
ent approach from anything we have previously encountered.
Not only does he refer to earlier commentators, especially the
Fathers, but he makes explicit use of grammars and lexica.

Much of his long note of seven pages is taken up with detail.
He observes that the letter begins like all Paul's letters with
thanksgiving, though he does not comment on the particular
form in this letter or on the renewal of the thanksgiving at 1:15-
16. In grammatical matters he discusses the missing copula
with 'blessed . . .', the order of the words in this phrase, the
distinction between the verbal adjective $\epsilon \dot{\upsilon}\lambda o\gamma\eta\tau\acute{o}\varsigma$ and the
participle $\epsilon \dot{\upsilon}\lambda o\gamma\eta\mu\acute{\epsilon}\nu o\varsigma$. He notes that 'the God and Father of
our Lord Jesus Christ' is a common New Testament formula
but says that if God and Father were one phrase we should
expect a $\tau\epsilon$ $\kappa\alpha\acute{\iota}$. Interestingly he does not draw any christological
conclusion from his discussion. He is the first to show himself
aware of a variant reading, the omission of $\dot{\epsilon}\nu$ before $X\rho\iota\sigma\tau\hat{\omega}$
but does not accept it. Pointing out the aorist participle he
relates it to the once-for-all sending of Christ. He seems to be
aware of the unusual double meaning of 'bless' in Greek and
says it comes from the Septuagint but he does not make any
further attempt to account for it. 'Us' is not used of Paul alone
but of believers; any distinction that its meaning may hold first
appears in v. 11. He rejects any idea that 'spiritual' is used to
distinguish the present gifts of God from those of the Old
Testament; the word designates the blessings as the work of the
Holy Spirit. He devotes considerable space to 'the heavenlies'
which, noting parallels, he argues refer to heaven but not to a
'super-heaven' above the ordinary heaven nor to heaven as the
place where God is when he blesses. The blessings we receive
are those of a higher world for God has given us in Christ every
spiritual blessing which is in heaven.

Harless set the terms of the discussion for the next century.
Different commentators assess details differently and discuss

details Harless overlooked but with Harless the historical-critical method has now taken over and determines the course of the discussion. Succeeding writers are normally briefer and their selection of the points they discuss indicates their interests but even those who set out to write 'practical' or exhortatory commentaries cannot escape discussion of some of the detail; and if they do not explicitly discuss it they have read it and have made decisions which are incorporated in their writing. However it ought not to be assumed that the historical-critical method has taken full control; even those who use it most thoroughly still employ non-critical arguments to settle critical points. Thus J. Eadie[15] defends the linking of the genitive 'of our Lord Jesus Christ' to God on theological grounds as well as grammatical. J. Macpherson[16] includes a long discussion of the orthodoxy of the phrase taken as a unit.

The issue which commentators find most difficult is the understanding of 'spiritual blessing in the heavenlies (the great majority now take this locally) in Christ'. Thus Macpherson[17] writes:

> The atmosphere in which we live and breathe becomes heavenly . . . For us this heaven is at first a state — simply the reflection of our heavenliness of soul; at last, it will be realised as a place, where condition and locality perfectly correspond. Meanwhile, we have days of heaven upon earth, in proportion as our conversation, our way of life is in heaven.

The best known explanation is probably that of J. B. Lightfoot for it is regularly quoted by others: 'the heaven which lies within and about the true Christian'.[18] J. A. Robinson[19] is deserving of a little more attention since he both writes on this

---

[15] *A Commentary on the Greek Text of the Epistle of Paul to the Ephesians* (London and Glasgow, 1854).

[16] *Commentary on St Paul's Epistle to the Ephesians* (Edinburgh 1892).

[17] Ibid., p. 120.

[18] *Notes on Epistles of St Paul* (London, 1904) p. 312.

[19] J. A. Robinson, *St Paul's Epistle to the Ephesians* (London, 1903).

point at greater length than most and gives an exposition as well as exegesis of the passage. He begins by distinguishing the blessing of the Old Testament as primarily 'a material prosperity' from that of the New Covenant which 'is in another region: the region not of the body, but of the spirit' and argues that the reference in 'spiritual' is not to the Holy Spirit but to the human. The 'heavenlies' are a 'region of ideas, rather than locality' (p. 20), '. . . the sphere of spiritual activities: that immaterial region, the "unseen universe", which lies behind the world of sense' (p. 21). The phrase 'in Christ' 'belongs to the same supra-sensual region of ideas to which the two preceding phrases testify' (p. 24). It should be noted that Robinson unlike many earlier commentators examines each phrase in some detail before coming to his conclusions. He and similar commentators realise the need to make some sense out of this difficult passage. They do this by reducing the terms to earthly concepts. It is a kind of demythologisation but made in a platonic rather than a gnostic or existentialist framework.

It is worthy of note that four major commentaries appeared in eight years at the turn of the century: E. Haupt, 1897; T. K. Abbott, 1897; J. A. Robinson, 1903; P. Ewald, 1905. No other commentary approaches these in understanding or learning until the first edition of H. Schlier (1957). We must however mention one, J. O. F. Murray.[20] Though not a major commentary it treated in some detail issues which were to become prominent as time went by. He has a relatively lengthy note on $\epsilon\dot{\upsilon}\lambda o\gamma\acute{\epsilon}\omega$ in dependence on F. J. A. Hort's 1 Peter;[21] he notes that the word's double meaning comes via the Septuagint from the Hebrew *brk*. Observing the frequent appearance of the phrase 'in Christ' in Ephesians he has a long note about it in his introduction (pp. lxii-lxxvi), making extensive use of the

---

[20] *Ephesians* (Cambridge Greek Testament, Cambridge, 1914).
[21] *The First Epistle of St Peter, i, I-ii.* 17 (London, 1898).

work of A. Deissmann[22] on the phrase; although Deissmann's work was published in 1892 it is surprising how long it took for its ideas to find a place in commentaries. Since Murray believed Paul wrote Ephesians he does not discuss possible differences of meaning from the genuine Paulines.

With H. Schlier[23] we begin a new batch of major commentaries (J. Gnilka, 1971; M. Barth, 1974; R. Schnackenburg, 1982) which have benefitted from new avenues of discussion in the general study of the New Testament and as a result are no longer content to repeat old themes but attempt to look anew at the verse. We give the major attention to Schlier, not because it provides the correct answers but because it first opened up the new areas. The first edition appeared in 1957; I have used the seventh of 1971.

We now find greater attention being paid to the form of the benediction than formerly. It is traced back to the Old Testament through inter-testamental Judaism. The tendency to examine 'forms' began with the gospels but spread into other areas after World War II. The benediction form is now seen as clearly distinct from the thanksgiving and commentators begin to note that Ephesians possesses both. But while v. 3a is a benediction form the whole of vv. 3-14, or at least vv. 3-10, are recognised as a 'eulogy form'. This form is found also in 2 Cor. 1:3 ff., and 1 Pet. 1:3 ff. as well as widely in contemporary Jewish literature. Closely associated with this is a discussion of the actual structure of vv. 3-14. So far as I can trace, M. Dibelius[24] was the first to introduce this but it had been under consideration for some years in the academic journals, apparently stemming from an article by M. T. Innitzer in 1904.[25]

---

[22] *Die neutestamentliche Formel 'In Christo Jesu'* (Marbug, 1892).

[23] *Der Brief an die Epheser* (Düsseldorf, 1957).

[24] *An die Kolosser, Epheser, an Philemon* (Tübingen, 1st ed. 1913; 3rd ed. 1953).

[25] 'Der Hymnus in Eph. 1, 3-14,' *Zeitschrift für Theologie und Kirche* 28 (1904) 612 ff.

Is Eph. 1:3-14 a hymn? If so, was the hymn written by the author of Ephesians or did he use an existing entity? If it is not a hymn does it have any kind of structure and how is it to be categorised? We may discern here not only the influence of form-criticism but also and more importantly the revival of interest in the twentieth century in liturgy. If liturgies appear reasonably early in the history of the church can we trace them back into the New Testament itself? Coincident with this and affecting it has been the attempt to discover pre-written elements in the New Testament. While this may have originated in the desire to reach some primitive kerygma it quickly took over as a subject in itself. Consequently almost all contemporary commentaries have a section on these issues. An examination of them would suggest that opinion has gradually swung against any idea of a pre-existing hymn incorporated in Ephesians chapter 1 towards the use by the author of liturgical language. Schlier's actual phrase is often quoted by others: in the eulogy we deal 'mit einem einheitlichen, ad hoc geschaffenen, hymnus *artigen* Abschnitt in rhythmischer Kunstprosa' (p. 41). Evidence drawn from Qumran has reinforced this conclusion. Here we may note how new discoveries of material have also helped in the solution of old problems. The papyri found at the close of last century threw much light on language and grammar while Qumran and Nag Hammadi have helped rather in respect of concepts.

The examination of other letters of the Pauline corpus suggested that their introductory section set out the pattern for what was later to be discussed in the body of the letter. Thus attempts have been made to relate 1:3-14 to the succeeding main section of the letter. In the case of Ephesians this seems to have begun with an article by C. Maurer,[26] or at least he was the first to study the idea seriously and work it out in detail.[27]

---

[26]'Der Hymnus von Epheser I als Schlüssel zum ganzen Briefe', *EvT* 11 (1951) 151-72.
[27]Cf. Bengel, supra.

Looking at more individual points we find that there is still diversity of opinion as to the reference of the aorist in the participle translated as 'has blessed'. While a connection with baptism had often been conjectured N. A. Dahl[28] appears to have been the first to attempt to connect the letter as a whole to the sacrament. This connection, and also one to the eucharist, is now more generally made. It has probably been spurred on by the revived interest in all denominations in worship coupled with ecumenical discussion of the sacraments.

The question of authorship has not been of great importance in the exegesis of our verse with the exception of the discussion of the phrase 'in Christ'. We noted earlier Murray's long treatment of this theme. Discussions of the phrase itself now usually exclude the material from Ephesians on the ground that it is non-Pauline. So beginning with J. A. Allan[29] commentators tend to look at the use of the phrase in the epistle apart from its use by Paul generally. It cannot be said that this has led to any general agreement on what it means in this verse.

The more recent discussion of 'spiritual' has seen agreement that it must be related in some way to the Holy Spirit but with the revived interest in charismatic gifts in the sixties of this century commentators have been more careful to say that its use in v. 3 cannot be restricted to such gifts. So far as I can see, this denial comes to the fore first in M. Simajoki.[30] It again shows how outside pressures affect exegesis.

The most difficult phrase in the verse has always been 'the heavenlies'. Earlier commentators had been content to introduce verses from other parts of the New Testament which included the word 'heaven' or to examine the way in which the particular form of the word was used in Ephesians. Schlier

[28]N. A. Dahl *et alii, Kurze Auslegung des Epheserbriefes* (Göttingen, 1965) p. 11.
[29]'The "In Christ" Formula in Ephesians', *NTS* 5 (1958/9) 54-62.
[30]Dahl, op. cit. p. 104.

however was able to make use of the rich field of material unearthed by the *religionsgeschichtliche Schule*. Dibelius had already availed himself of it as had Schlier in earlier work. The latter now utilised it in his commentary in conjunction with an existentialist approach to create a new interpretation. 'Heaven' is that which gives transcendance to life, gives a man a width and depth of existence and allows him to stand outside himself. Since the 'powers' exist in heaven this means that there is more than one possibility of existence for man and he is continually challenged to choose between them. Each heaven, that of Christ and that of the powers, claims him. It cannot be said that this existentialist approach has won over a majority of commentators but it has affected much writing. 'The world-picture' of Paul (Schlier takes Ephesians to be Pauline) which he deduces has also of course been controverted.

With regard to the phrase itself one other approach should also be mentioned. A. T. Lincoln[31] is in the process of producing a commentary on Ephesians and we may assume that this will contain the views he has promulgated elsewhere.[32] Unlike Schlier he has gone to Jewish rather than to Hellenistic material and explained the phrase in terms of the two ages. 'Paul conceives of the two ages as coexistent, and in this period of overlap the believer is regarded as involved in two spheres of existence simultaneously' (p. 48). We see here in this limited area traces of the wider conflict between two different general approaches to the New Testament, one dominated by the attempt to elucidate difficulties from the Hellenistic field (Schlier) and the other from the Jewish (Lincoln).

I hope the preceding survey, short as it has been, has justified the title of this paper. We have seen how questions arising in areas exterior to our verse have affected its interpretation — the non-Ephesian factors which affect the interpretation of

---

[31]In the series Word Biblical Commentary.
[32]'A Re-Examination of "the heavenlies" in Ephesians', *NTS* 19 (1972/3) 468-83.

Ephesians. Commentaries which treat the same issue differently or treat different issues are written because scholars are invited by the circumstances in which they stand to pose different questions to the text. Consequently new aspects have been uncovered and at the same time new answers given to previously recognised problems. Techniques and methods developed for the study of other parts of the New Testament have been extended to apply to our text, and of course to all texts. For what we have attempted to show in respect of Eph. 1:3 could be equally demonstrated in respect of a thousand other verses. There is then no such thing as a neutral exegesis. The questions we pose to any text have been created for us in the first instance by those who have previous studied that text. We either agree with them or are forced to examine further and justify our disagreement. But our environment, and I use this term in its widest sense, leads us also to ask new questions and to see the material in new ways. This can happen as new philosophies come to the fore or as new interests, e.g. in worship and liturgy, are raised by others for us, or as new methods of examining the text, e.g. form-criticism, are transferred from one part of the New Testament to other parts.

The main difficulty in the verse has always been the reference to the 'heavenlies'. At first many commentators simply ignored the past tense of the participle 'blessed' and thought of future blessings in heaven. Others who took seriously the past tense have been forced to interpret it within the various frameworks of Platonism, gnosticism, existentialism, Jewish two-age ideas. Platonic and existentialist interpretations have been attempts to put the term into words which readers could understand(?). It cannot be said that they have been successful but then such interpretations quickly pass out of date and require to be carried through again for each generation. Perhaps commentators should not attempt them but be content merely to explain first century ideas in terms of other first century ideas (i.e. the two ages) within a first century background. But do those who restrict themselves in this way really get to the heart of the matter? Here we come to the centre of the hermeneutical discussion and must desist.

9

PAUL AND THECLA

The approach to the interpretation of Scripture has varied through the period of the church. This can be seen most easily when we take a text or brief passage and examine the different ways it has been understood since the time of its original writing. Difficulties in the text have always been observed but when they have not been ignored they have been treated obliquely rather than directly, attention being focussed in some way or other on anything but what the text actually says. Texts have also been used to advance particular theological points of view without regard to their main meaning. We may perhaps illustrate this with two verses in Acts which have not received all the attention they deserve, their neglect probably arising because of their absence from the main manuscripts, of which more later. This absence itself may have come about through the increasing rejection of women as ministers of the gospel from the second century onwards; this led to the suppression of information about them.[1] In English translation the verses in question run as follows:

> While Paul was still preaching the word and teaching in Ephesus Thecla whom he had converted in Iconium came to visit him. She worked with him for four months and then left hurriedly.

[1]Cf. Ben Witherington, *Women in the Earliest Churches* (SNTS Monograph Series 59), Chambridge, CUP, 1988, pp. 183ff.

The Fathers did not pay much attention to Acts and of the commentaries they wrote almost nothing has survived. The first of the great commentators was Origen; we do not even know if he wrote consecutively on Acts. Fortunately Jerome, who regularly depends on Origen, has preserved one brief quotation from him on these verses:

As hurriedly as Thecla left Paul will the Lord return.

Here as so often Origen ignores the context and general flow of the passage and concentrates on one item, in this case on the one word 'hurriedly'. (We shall see as we go on how much this word has dominated the exegesis.) And from this one word he draws a 'spiritual' conclusion which has nothing to do with the content of the passage. Typically he does not attempt to explain why Thecla left in such a hurry. Other Fathers regularly refer to Thecla but do not comment on our passage. Apparently she was held in great esteem because she remained a virgin (as we shall see later doubts are cast on this by some modern commentators) and daughters were frequently named after her.[2] Fuller details about her conversion and later activities were written up in the *Acts of Paul and Thecla*.[3] Its preservation indicates the high view held of her in the early church.

As we might expect some writers in the Middle Ages picked up the story and expanded it, but in an entirely different way from Origen. The authors of that period seem to be able to write indefinitely on verses if somehow they can allegorise them, and the theme of sexual love, if it could be introduced at all, was always grist to their mill. John of the Abbey of Ford in Devon wrote seven sermons on our brief passage (this shows that a copy of Acts containing it had reached England by his

[2]On Thecla's place in early church thought see D. R. Macdonald, *The Legend and the Apostle: The Battle for Paul in Story and Canon*, Philadelphia, Westminster, 1983.

[3]E.T. in E. Hennecke and W. Schneemelcher, *New Testament Apocrypha* (ed. R. McL. Wilson), vol. 2, London, Lutterworth, 1965, pp. 353ff.

period). There is only space to summarise what he wrote but anyone who has read his many sermons on the Song of Songs will be well placed to fill out this summary. He begins by saying that the true soul loves to visit its Lord in prayer as Thecla visited Paul. When with the Lord time passes quickly. There is much love. The solemn intercourse commences with words of endearment; then face is displayed to face; kisses follow; the left hand is under the head and the right hand devoted to holy fondling; there is ravishing enjoyment. Time passes quickly and the mind is engulfed in the timeless Lord. Yet the moment always comes when the bride must once again occupy herself with the mundane duties that belong to the housewife, and so remembering them she went off hurriedly to fulfil them.

We do not find much reference to the passage in the exegesis of the Reformers. This is a pity since with their insistence on the literal meaning of Scripture it would have been interesting to see what they made of it. Luther did not write a commentary on Acts but there is one brief allusion to the verses in the Table Talk. In answer to a question from Justus Jonas about the passage he responded

> Paul was no monk living apart from women. They came to him as they come to me. Neither I nor Paul reject them. We teach them and would have them marry us.

Calvin wrote commentaries on all the books of the New Testament except Revelation and the younger Scaliger said of this omission that it displayed his wisdom. The absence of a comment on our verses reveals the same sagacity. If a comment would be embarrassing it is better to say nothing.

The pietest Bengel wrote on all the New Testament; he is distinguished among commentators for the pungency and brevity of his exegesis and by his general unwillingness to deal with anything other than grammatical matters. Very occasionally he goes a little further. Here after drawing attention to a peculiarity in the use of one participle he adds

Thecla wished to be Mary, Paul wished her to be Martha.
Later Catholic exegetes point out that it was Bengel's Protestantism that led him into this error. Mary is the model for the
quiet contemplative and not for the active missionary.

We come now to the nineteenth and twentieth centuries
and the rise of the historical critical movement, and a whole
new range of problems comes to the fore. Attention is now
focused on what actually happened and there is a reluctance to
draw spiritual lessons. Since our text provides so little hard
information ample scope is given to ingenuity in relating it to
other parts of the Pauline corpus. It is only possible to outline
here general trends without referring to particular scholars.
While various solutions are proposed there is almost universal
agreement that these two verses in Acts led to the later writing
of the *Acts of Paul and Thecla* and many attempts are made to
discover the 'real Thecla' behind the legend.

Observing that Paul wrote most of the Corinthian correspondence while in Ephesus various writers speculate on the
way that correspondence was affected by Thecla's arrival and
sudden departure. 1 Cor. 7.36-38 with its reference to the way
a believer should treat his 'betrothed' (*parthenos*) has always
occasioned difficulties for exegetes. If Paul is suggesting there
that a man and a woman should be able to live together and
abstain from sexual intercourse this may be a conclusion he
drew from his own experience since that was the way he lived
with Thecla. He had no need to marry her for there was
nothing physical about their companionship. Support for this
view is supplied by one of the introductory sentences to the *Acts
of Paul and Thecla* which runs, 'Blessed are they who have wives
as if they had them not, for they shall inherit God'.[4]

In 1 Corinthians there is a notable clash between 11.1 ff.
which appears to permit ministerial activity on the part of

[4]Op. cit., p. 354.

women and 14.33-36 which requires them to keep silent in church gatherings. Tertullian says that in parts of the second century church it was believed that Paul had instructed Thecla to teach and baptise;[5] such advice from Paul can be supported from 1 Cor. 1.14-16 where Paul, though concerned that everyone should be baptised, does not appear to be worried as to the celebrant. Some modern commentators accordingly suggest that the hurried departure of Thecla fell between the writing of the two contradictory passages in 1 Corinthians. Paul's attitude to women had suddenly changed. But what led to this change? Had his attempt to maintain with Thecla a non-physical relationship failed and being a man he laid the blame on her? He therefore drove her away and realising the frailty of the female nature it was time women took a back seat. Thus having begun by encouraging women to lead in worship he now rejected such a role for them. It has been further conjectured that he later repented of this change in his attitude to women; it was this repentance which led to his desire to travel to Spain after his release from prison in Rome for he had heard Thecla was in Spain and wished to seek her forgiveness.

The majority of commentators however have approached the problem from Thecla's angle and asked what caused her sudden departure. Various theories have been proposed and these can only be briefly indicated here. (1) Paul's ability to sustain the non-physical relationship collapsed and Thecla fled fearing she would lose her virginity. (2) She and Paul were unable to maintain the non-physical nature of their togetherness and she became pregnant; in order to preserve Paul's reputation she fled from Corinth so that she could have the baby elsewhere and save Paul's reputation. (3) She had become pregnant by someone else and feared Paul would be blamed; realising the great task to which God had called him as apostle

[5] *De Baptismo* 1.17.

to the Gentiles she left so that his reputation would remain unsmirched. (4) Believing Paul's mind was slowly changing in respect of the place of women in the ministry and that there would soon be nothing he would permit her to do other than cook his meals she went off to an area where he could not control her and where she could continue in freedom her own God-given ministry. (5) She felt she was not getting a fair share of the ministerial work in Corinth and in order to exercise her full ministry she thought it better that she and Paul should separate. (6) On the whole these explanations are highly speculative and have been rejected, probably wisely, by most conservative scholars. These have sought to preserve both her reputation and that of Paul by finding a reason for her hurried departure in some cause just as likely to be true as any of those already outlined. They have suggested that perhaps her mother was taken seriously ill and needed nursing attention or had died and her father required her at home to look after him.

There is no need for us to choose between these various theories. Their existence clearly shows a very different way in which the direction of exegesis has moved in the last one hundred and fifty years in comparison to all the earlier period. Two more recent interpretations however deserve to be noted since both are dominated by considerations other than those of the historical critical method.

In the volume on Acts from the True Gospel Press (published in the deep south of the U.S.A.) the author points first to a poorly attested reading in two minor manuscripts and accepts it on the ground that it fits better with the general position of the New Testament in respect of the role of women in the church. This reading changes 'worked with Paul' to 'worked for Paul'. After pointing this out the commentator continues

> Thecla was a good woman who in her love for the gospel took care of Paul, just as women had ministered to Jesus. She cooked for him, washed

and mended his clothes; thus fulfilling her womanly function she freed him for the task that God has given only to men, that of the preaching of the gospel. She left him when she was summoned home by a sudden crisis there.

The other interpretation comes from the commentary on Acts published by the feminist Amazon Press. It commences by pointing out the sexist nature of Paul's views on women. Thecla having read or heard about Paul's views as expressed in Gal. 3.28 joined him in Corinth believing that he accepted the equality of men and women. She quickly found him intolerable. He kept telling her to obey him since he, and every other male, was her head. The writer goes on to point out:

> In addition Paul was jealous of her success as a preacher. Where he converted tens, she converted hundreds; all whether converted by him or her preferred to be baptized by her. The break came finally when he began to treat her as a sex object and not as a fellow worker in the gospel. To forestall his advances she hurriedly left Ephesus so as to be able to continue the Lord's work in fresh fields.

Taking all these interpretations together two lessons are suggested for budding exegetes: the twin dangers of permitting the imagination to take over where there is no information and of permitting presuppositions to rule what is deduced.

10

MADE TO MEASURE OR OFF THE PEG

For Roberr Davidson on his retirement

After the death and resurrection of Jesus the first Christians needed to explain his significance to themselves and to others. For this purpose they had available in the Jewish faith and in the culture of the ancient world the various terms and concepts used to describe important people ('off the peg'); they also created others ('made to measure') which they thought suitable. Among existing terms 'Christ' was peculiar to Judaism, but 'king' was more widely used. When terms already in use were adopted they often had to be qualified when applied to Jesus, just as clothes off the peg often need slight modifications if they are to fit. Thus both Christ and king had to be evacuated of political meaning if they were to be suitable.

A term initially chosen might later turn out to be unsuitable for general use. This is what happened to 'Christ'. To a Jew it was a religious term; to non-Jews it meant nothing, or, more precisely, it may have suggested someone who had a warm bath and then rubbed oil into (anointed) himself or herself. While to instructed Christians it must still have retained its religious significance it quickly degenerated in ordinary usage into what we would describe as a 'surname', that of Jesus, Jesus Christ. Because of its non-religious connotation for Gentiles it is not found so often in the New Testament by itself but usually linked to the personal name Jesus. As time went on and its Jewish meaning was grasped it regained its significance, though today many who use or hear it have no idea of its full significance. 'King' on the other hand was a term which could be used almost everywhere in the ancient world and would be understood. Another term which was taken up and used briefly but later abandoned was that of prophet. Like the prophets of old Jesus stood in opposition to the established order and like many of them suffered for his stand. Yet as a description of Jesus it was one that was not a good fit, indeed in the eyes of the growing church it was a bad fit.

Other terms were also taken up, e.g. son of God. We do not need to discuss when or how this came into use. It was probably not a term which would have leaped to the mind of a Jew to describe someone of importance in the same way as Christ. It might have been used to signify someone with charismatic ability or someone who was specially obedient to God. Since Jesus was a healer and appeared to seek God's will it was an appropriate term, yet once in use it required considerable definition if misunderstanding was to be avoided. God was not the father of Jesus in the same way as an earthly father was father to his son. So we find in the christological controversies of the early church considerable attention given to defining precisely what was meant when Jesus was called son of God. As a term it is one which has survived and this may simply be because in the early days it could be appreciated by Gentile converts since in many of their religions it already had a religious application and also because it describes a basic human relationship which everyone knows something about.

A term which did come into use in the early church presumably because it was in use in contemporary Palestine but later fell out of use was 'son of man'. It appears all through the Gospels but not in the Pauline letters and it does not feature in the later christological controversies. Scholars today have considerable difficulty in explaining it, and the first Christians in non-Palestinian areas may have found themselves equally puzzled by it and so dropped it from use. Curiously its use was

revived with the rise of the liberal theology of the late nineteenth and early twentieth centuries; here it was used to denote
the humanity of Jesus, its first century apocalyptic connections
now forgotten.

These are all terms which lay to hand and were therefore 'off
the peg'. Were there no terms which the first Christians put
into use but which had no previous religious history, or if they
had a previous religious connection it lay outside Judaism and
were therefore in the true sense 'made to measure'? Clearly any
term brought into use must have had some previous cultural
history for as a word or set of words it will suggest a concept and
the concept would not be used if it did not have a meaning and
a meaning which could be appreciated by its readers or hearers.
In both Acts (3.15; 5.31) and Hebrews (2.10; 12.2) we have
Christ denoted as 'pioneer', *archēgos*. This is a term which has
been derived from contemporary non-Christian religion but it
is also in itself a powerful metaphor; despite this it is not a term
which has had a consistent and regular use in Christianity,
though the conception of Jesus as a leader is often used. But
because it was a term already used in at least some other
contemporary religions we must allocate it to the category 'off
the peg'.

Another concept, for this is here a better way of describing
it than term, was that of reconciliation. This does not appear
to have been previously of great religious significance though
politically important; it is used in theology to cover an area for
which there were already a number of terms: redemption,
expiation, propitiation, salvation. In contrast with these, all of
which have a religious background in a number of faiths, and
all the terms we have already considered, this must be placed
in the 'made to measure' category. Though found in 2
Maccabees (1.5; 5.20; 7.33) it has the sense there of God being
reconciled to humanity and not as in the New Testament of
humanity as reconciled to God. It was however a term widely

used in social and political life and appears in the New Testament used with general significance (see Matt. 24; 1 Cor. 7.11); it therefore could be understood by anyone. Paul seems to have been the first to introduce it into Christianity. What Christ did in dying was used by God to reconcile men to himself. On one occasion Christ himself is spoken of as the reconciler (Eph. 2.16). Coming into use then at almost the beginning it has continued as a popular description; there must be few churches where the term is not heard regularly.

Unlike expiation, propitiation and similar terms its meaning can be easily grasped. It is a powerful metaphor and for that reason requires careful definition. Curiously this never seems to have been carried out (contrast the attention given to 'son of God' in the early church). In an industrial dispute someone is called in to reconcile workers and management; the case is argued out before the reconciler and he or she persuades both parties to move toward one another from their original positions by surrendering some of their claims. But no one would suggest that Christ seeks to make God and humanity modify their original claims on one another. Again in daily life we may say that we become reconciled to a situation so that we can live with it; but neither God nor Christ is regarded as becoming reconciled in that kind of way to the human situation. We also speak of reconciling two accounts of a situation; two eyewitnesses may produce slightly different stories in relation to it and we have to pick between their respective points of view to produce an acceptable account; but our reconciliation with God is not one in which his view of us and our view of ourselves or of him have to be brought into harmony. A metaphor like reconciliation which awakens so many echoes in people's minds has always to be carefully handled lest the wrong nuance be produced.

Another description of Christ emerged in a more roundabout way. Paul was apparently the first to call the church

Christ's body. If each Christian is a part or member of that body is Christ one also and if so what special position does he have? We can imagine the question being asked and in the later Paulines (Ephesians, Colossians) the answer comes: he is the head. At first sight this might seem to be very little different from describing him as its lord or king (the king and head of the church) but when we look at the way it is used we see that because, unlike king, it connects Christ closely to the church it has another sense: Christ as the source of the life of the church (Eph. 4.15, 16; Col. 2.19). Here then we have quite clearly a term 'made to measure'.

Both 'reconciliation' and 'headship' are wide metaphors and applicable in a number of different areas. This is not true in the same way of our next examples. In 2 Corinthians Paul pleads with the Corinthians to contribute more generously to the fund he is raising for the church in Jerusalem. It is unnecessary to follow through the arguments he uses to persuade them; most of them are prudential. At one point, however, he says to them that they 'know the grace of the our Lord Jesus Christ, that though he was rich, yet for your sake he became poor. so that by his poverty you might become rich' (8.9). Here is a doctrine of the incarnation but instead of being expressed in the philosophical or religious terms to which we are accustomed it is cast in financial terms. Paul has put it in this way because he is talking to the Corinthian about money and thinks he can do it more effectively if he describes Christ in financial terms. Is this not truly an understanding 'made to measure'?

Our second example comes from the same letter. The Corinthians have accused Paul of reneging on a promise to visit them and he denies that he has been vacillating; it was for their own good that he did not come. The nature of truth is at issue and Paul introduces Christ to support his position: 'For the son of God . . . was not Yes and No; but in him it is always Yes.'

Christ is then the Yes or Amen of God (1.15-21). Little use has been made of this concept in christology but it fits appropriately into a context where truth is at issue.

Clothes wear out and this is true both of those off the peg and those made to measure, though the latter probably last longer because they fit better. This however may not be true in respect of descriptions of the significance of Christ. Clearly some wore out very quickly, for instance 'son of man'. When it was revived last century it was revived because a new meaning was read into it. Others have endured; amongst them have been many of those drawn from Judaism and from ordinary life. This is not surprising in respect of those drawn from daily life if they are sufficiently basic to be understood in most cultures. So far as terms drawn from Judaism go it is again natural because there is a continuity between Christianity and Judaism and Christianity can never cut itself off from its traditional religious source. So 'Christ' has survived and continues in steady use, though I am not sure it is always understood: I thought it was until I conducted a Bible study group in one of our leading well-to-do congregations when I discovered that at least half the members, and these included university graduates, thought it was another word for 'crucified'! The words of preachers may arouse very different ideas in the minds of their hearers from what the preachers think!

The description of Jesus as son of God has also clearly survived but for a very different reason, not because it was a necessary term in Judaism but because it employs a relationship with which we are all familiar; men certainly experience it in a different way from women but women have some idea of what it means. For very similar reasons 'reconciliation' continues in use and, at least in theological circles, 'head'. But there are other terms which are beginning to show signs of wear. This is probably true in the case of 'king', and that not simply because there is a queen and no king in the United

Kingdom. The function of a king has changed entirely from Biblical times. He, or she, is no longer a person in whom great authority is vested. Generally where monarchs still exist they do so as figureheads. Real power lies elsewhere. Perhaps so long as monarchs continue in some parts of the world and fairy stories in which they feature in the traditional way are still told to children the image will not disappear. But it becomes less effective, especially in countries which do not have kings or queens but elected heads of government. This is not to say that the conception of one who rules over others has disappeared; we use other terms for it like President or Prime Minister.

Another traditional image may be on the way out, that of the shepherd. It is an image drawn from both the Old Testament and several other religions of the period and therefore was very valuable as a description of Jesus in the early days and in rural cultures ever since. As far as the ancient world went it was 'off the peg'. But is it as well-known today? Ours is not a rural culture. So when preachers refer to it they regularly begin by explaining the agricultural function of the shepherd in the ancient world. The image has however not merely changed in relation to its function; shepherds no longer go before their sheep and know them by name, but drive them from behind with dogs; in many parts of the world the image is disappearing altogether. More than that there are parts of the world where it does not merely not exist today but never did exist. Eskimos have no knowledge of sheep or shepherds and those who use the term with them need to explain it in detail (we at least know what sheep look like and a little about how they behave) before it can carry any meaning. 'Shepherd' when it first came into use may have been a suit of clothes off the peg but as anyone who is not normally built will know there are shops where it is impossible to get something off the peg that will even come near a fit and 'shepherd' will just not fit an Eskimo.

When we looked at the images that the first Christians

manufactured for themselves, the 'made to measure' images, we saw that they were, roughly speaking, of two types; there were the more or less universal images of reconciliation and headship and there were the very much narrower images of Christ as rich and then poor and as the 'Yes' of God; these images because of their narrowness could not be widely used.

The two types, 'off the peg' and 'made to measure', have continued through the centuries of church thought and new images have regularly appeared. The basic image of 'honour' in relation to the death of Christ came into being in the late middle ages under the influence of 'knightly honour'. This was an image introduced to suit its period and culture and it is not for us who belong to a different period and culture to criticise its effectiveness. More importantly we do not need to trace the rise and fall of the many images which have appeared for a time and then been discarded; instead we ought to move directly to our own time. There can be no doubt about the need for the development of new 'made to measure' images.

Lively preachers have always created the narrower type of image. Sometimes they have derived them from current affairs as reflected in the media. At other times they have been produced because they fitted the situation of the congregation. How many ministers called on to address a group of sportsmen (I use 'men' deliberately) have not talked about the need to play together as a team with Christ as the captain who controls it all. Perhaps it is a useful image and does make a point relative to the situation as Paul's poverty image of Christ in relation to the need for a larger collection did but it has its hazards. I remember in the early days of women ministers seeing a cartoon in an American theological journal where one woman member of the congregation says to another as she sees their first woman minister mount the pulpit steps 'Now we'll have an end to Jesus as the quarterback who calls the plays'. These narrow images need then to be kept to their immediate context and not used in areas where they are not relevant to all the hearers.

But a much greater hazard exists: trivialisation. A minister in a children's address once spoke to them about loofahs; a loofah, he said, was useful in the bath because it enabled you to clean parts of your back you otherwise couldn't get at; it enabled you to do something you couldn't otherwise do by yourself; now, boys and girls, he concluded, Jesus is just like that; he can do things for you that you can't do for yourself. It may be in accord with Pauline views on 'works' but what a trivialisation! A loofah christology can hardly be considered a serious contribution to theological speculation. Yet with the dangers in mind we need to keep on producing these 'made to measure' images to make a point and then be ready to discard them for ever. They probably get home to people in a way more theological terms may not. It is not for me to suggest possible images, not because I live as an academic in an ivory tower and not in the real world, but because they must emerge from an actual situation and will not do this until the situation exists. Paul had many other and more profound ways of talking about Jesus than in financial terms.

Images like that of the team captain may be said to be situationally conditioned; there are also wider images which can be regarded as culturally conditioned in that they suit a wide range of situations and may even be useful in more than one culture. A description of Jesus which is in constant theological use today and may be said to be 'off the peg', even though it is not found in Scripture, because the image is drawn from outside theology and has a wide application in some cultures is 'representative'. Jesus is God's representative; Jesus is our representative. As a term it seems to come from the political arena as king once did. In that sense also it is an image 'off the peg' rather than one 'made to measure'. But it has of course an entirely different perspective from king. Since it is widely used in daily life we need to think out what we mean by it when we use it in a Christian context. A business firm appoints representatives to further the sale of its products. If God is taken to be the firm then Jesus may be thought of in a limited and legitimate way as his representative; we know God through him. The difficulties in the term appear more clearly when we think of Jesus as our representative — he represents us in his death on the cross. It is true to say that a member of Parliament represents his constituency, that is 'us', at Westminster, but he did not appoint himself to represent us; we appointed him. So when we speak of Christ as our representative we must mean something quite different from the idea of elected representative. In some trade unions delegates from local branches are mandated as representatives of the branch to vote in a particular way on certain issues at the union's general meeting; we did not mandate Christ to die for us on the cross. When we use this term we need to be careful lest to people untrained in theology it suggests the wrong image. Yet it is a good image for in some way Jesus associates himself with our lives and we associate ourselves with what he does.

Another phrase which has come into use more recently is Jesus as 'the man for others'. Leaving aside for the moment the male orientation of this image (we could change it to 'the one for others') it also has its value and its drawbacks. In earlier days all thinking began from God. He was the initial concept. Today almost all thinking begins from the human situation; it is therefore natural to use a description of Jesus in 'human terms', a christology from below. It is moreover one that no matter what their theological orientation all Christian thinkers can use from time to time. It expresses clearly that Jesus's existence was not selfish but that he put others before himself. Its drawback will be for some that it leaves Jesus entirely on the human plane, something which is vividly seen in the way an image originally applied to Jesus is now more widely applied to others.

It also suffers from its male orientation. The approach to theology from fresh angles has always yielded new images. We may expect feminist theology to do this; it is too early yet to speak of any image universally acceptable to all feminist theologians, let alone their male colleagues. The attempt to produce such images suffers from the male orientation of Scripture and the way male images have dominated theology so that male theologians find it difficult to see the value of feminist images. On the other hand liberation theology can begin more easily from Scripture in that the people of God in the Old Testament story were often oppressed and many were poor, something which was also true of many New Testament Christians. The images of Jesus as the liberator and revolutionary are not then so far away from the starting point in Scripture. But they do not fit so readily into the culture of Western Europe where as explanations of Jesus they may seem to be remote and useless, if not positively harmful, in the eyes of some who are politically conservative. That would not however be true of feminist imagery, or at least it should not be since women form the larger section of most congregations. Yet if one listens carefully to preachers their imagery still continues to be male oriented. Perhaps now that more women are entering the ministry this will change. We should expect that in time both 'off the peg' and 'made to measure' images will come from this area and assist us to understand; it is not however for a male theologian to say what they ought to be, less still to rule them out as irrelevant before they come into use.

Christian thought can never be static. There are no final terms which offer a full, complete and absolute christology, not even the term that seems most basic, 'son of God', if there are languages, as there are, which do not contain words for either father or son. All Christian thinking must be carried out in the thinking of the cultures and situations where it is being proclaimed, and if it is to come home in each situation and culture there must be a readiness to accept new clothing whether it be off the peg or made to measure. To put this another way: if the New Testament is to be understood today it needs to be extended so that new variations are created of its main theme, a theme which is understood through the primary variations which form the New Testament.

AUTHOR INDEX

BIBLICAL REFERENCE
(only those commented on are listed)

SUBJECT INDEX